Getting Skills Right

I0047730

Career Guidance for Adults in Latin America

OECD

BETTER POLICIES FOR BETTER LIVES

This work is published under the responsibility of the Secretary-General of the OECD. The opinions expressed and arguments employed herein do not necessarily reflect the official views of OECD member countries.

This document, as well as any data and map included herein, are without prejudice to the status of or sovereignty over any territory, to the delimitation of international frontiers and boundaries and to the name of any territory, city or area.

The statistical data for Israel are supplied by and under the responsibility of the relevant Israeli authorities. The use of such data by the OECD is without prejudice to the status of the Golan Heights, East Jerusalem and Israeli settlements in the West Bank under the terms of international law.

Note by Turkey
The information in this document with reference to "Cyprus" relates to the southern part of the Island. There is no single authority representing both Turkish and Greek Cypriot people on the Island. Turkey recognises the Turkish Republic of Northern Cyprus (TRNC). Until a lasting and equitable solution is found within the context of the United Nations, Turkey shall preserve its position concerning the "Cyprus issue".

Note by all the European Union Member States of the OECD and the European Union
The Republic of Cyprus is recognised by all members of the United Nations with the exception of Turkey. The information in this document relates to the area under the effective control of the Government of the Republic of Cyprus.

Please cite this publication as:
OECD (2021), *Career Guidance for Adults in Latin America*, Getting Skills Right, OECD Publishing, Paris, *https://doi.org/10.1787/4eaf4996-en*.

ISBN 978-92-64-69305-0 (print)
ISBN 978-92-64-38509-2 (pdf)

Getting Skills Right
ISSN 2520-6117 (print)
ISSN 2520-6125 (online)

Foreword

The world of work is changing. Digitalisation, automation and globalisation are having a profound impact on the type and quality of jobs that are available and the skills required to perform them. The extent to which individuals, firms and economies can reap the benefits of these changes will depend critically on the ability of individuals to maintain and acquire relevant skills and adapt to a changing labour market over their working careers.

Career guidance for adults is a fundamental policy lever to motivate adults to train and help address the challenges brought about by rapidly changing skill needs. Such services are particularly important in the context of the COVID-19 pandemic and its aftermath, as many adults have lost jobs and require assistance navigating their career options in the changed labour market.

To explore this issue, the OECD Directorate for Employment, Labour and Social Affairs has undertaken an ambitious programme of work on the functioning, effectiveness and resilience of adult career guidance systems across countries. As part of this project, the OECD carried out an online survey in nine countries (Argentina, Brazil, Chile, France, Germany, Italy, Mexico, New Zealand and the United States) to better understand the user experience of adults with career guidance, and any barriers adults might face in accessing these services. This report focusses on the results of the Latin American countries that participated in the survey (Argentina, Brazil, Chile and Mexico), building on the OECD's earlier report on "Career Guidance for Adults in a Changing World of Work". It also leverages information on career guidance policies collected through a series of interviews with practitioners and policy makers in Latin America, as well as a questionnaire sent to Ministries of Employment and Education in the four countries.

This report was prepared by Karolin Killmeier, Magdalena Burtscher, and Katharine Mullock (project lead) from the Directorate for Employment, Labour and Social Affairs, under the supervision of Glenda Quintini (Skills team manager) and Mark Keese (Head of the Skills and Employability Division). Sapphire Han provided statistical assistance. Useful comments were provided by colleagues in the Skills and Employability Division in the OECD Directorate for Employment, Labour and Social Affairs.

This report is published under the responsibility of the Secretary General of the OECD. It was carried out with financial assistance from the JPMorgan Chase Foundation. The views expressed in this report should not be taken to reflect the official position of the JPMorgan Chase Foundation or OECD member countries.

Table of contents

FIGURES

TABLES

Follow OECD Publications on:

http://twitter.com/OECD_Pubs

http://www.facebook.com/OECDPublications

http://www.linkedin.com/groups/OECD-Publications-4645871

http://www.youtube.com/oecdilibrary

http://www.oecd.org/oecddirect/

Executive summary

Labour markets in Latin American countries have been hit hard by the COVID-19 pandemic. Working hours dropped by 16% during 2020, and low-skilled adults are among those most affected by rising unemployment. The crisis is likely to accelerate the adoption of digital technologies in the region. Without adequate support to individuals, these changes could durably worsen labour market outcomes in Latin American countries, where income inequality is already among the highest in the world and rates of unemployment and informality are high.

In this context, professional career guidance can help adults understand the risks to their jobs, navigate the evolving labour market and upskill and retrain in high-demand skills. Some 57% of adults in Latin America do not train and do not want to, and this share is well above the OECD average (49%). Lack of awareness about the benefits of training or difficulties finding suitable training opportunities may be behind this low interest in training, especially among low-skilled adults. Ideally, career guidance informs individuals about training and job opportunities, and empowers them to make decisions about their lifelong career development and learning that align with their personal interests as well as labour market demand. Evidence suggests that career guidance can have a positive impact on learning outcomes, training participation, and employment outcomes like finding a job or getting a promotion.

Career guidance for adults as conceived above, however, is still rare in the Latin American context. More common are vocational guidance programmes for young people or labour intermediation services for adults.

To understand the experiences of adults with career guidance and the barriers they face to access these services, the OECD conducted the online Survey of Career Guidance for Adults (SCGA). The four Latin American countries covered by the survey are Argentina, Brazil, Chile and Mexico. According to the survey, four out of ten adults in these Latin America countries have spoken to a career guidance professional in the previous five years. This share is comparable to other countries covered by the SCGA (France, Germany, Italy, New Zealand and the United States).

However, those who already face disadvantages in the labour market and who train less are least likely to use career guidance services. Among unemployed individuals in the Latin American countries covered by the survey, only 26% used career guidance in the previous 5 years, compared to 48% for employed individuals. This gap is almost non-existent across the non-Latin American countries in the survey. Other important gaps exist between high- and low-educated individuals (16 percentage points), prime-age (25-54) and older adults (over 54) (11 percentage points), as well as those in formal and informal employment (7 percentage points). These findings are worrying because they suggest that career guidance is not reaching those who most need it.

Indeed, adults in the Latin American countries covered by the survey who do not use career guidance are less likely to report that they did not need it, and are more likely to cite other barriers than those in non-Latin American countries. Of those adults who did not speak with a career guidance advisor over the past 5 years, only 37% did not feel the need to, a share which is considerably lower than the survey average across all countries (50%). Another 33% of adults reported not knowing career guidance services existed, which suggests a lack of awareness about career guidance services. Another possible barrier is cost: four out of ten users reported having paid partially or fully for career guidance services, which is higher than the survey average (3 out of 10). Unemployed adults in particular are much more likely to pay compared with unemployed adults in other countries. Less access to subsidised career guidance opportunities may be why adults in the Latin America countries in the survey are more likely than adults in other countries to rely on informal career support, like speaking to family and friends (35% versus 30% of adults).

The landscape of providers in Latin America is also different from elsewhere. Private career guidance providers are the dominant provider in Latin American countries covered in the survey serving 34% of adult users compared to 22% across all countries in the survey. By contrast, the public employment service plays a minor role, accounting for only 9% of users, compared with 27% of users across non-Latin American countries covered by the SCGA. The limited use of the public employment service in Latin America may be connected to low public funding as well as to built-in incentives for jobseekers to quickly find jobs rather than invest in career development for better long-term matches.

The COVID-19 pandemic has brought about considerable change in the use of career guidance in the Latin American countries covered in the survey: 51% of adults reported having used guidance services more often than usual, either because they had more time or because they were navigating the ongoing changes, and 17% reported having used it less. At the time of the survey, face-to-face delivery of career guidance was still most common (50% of users), though digital delivery channels were being expanded in most of the Latin American countries in this review. Each country has at least one online career guidance platform offering digital support such as labour market information, skills assessments, and job search advice, though many of these platforms could be strengthened.

Satisfaction with career guidance services is generally high, and a large majority of adults (82%) report having experienced an employment or training outcome – such as progressing in their current job, enrolling in training or education, or finding a new job – after having received career guidance. About 12% of adults reported that they had moved from informal to formal employment. Nevertheless, only a third of these adults attribute the positive outcomes to the career guidance they received. Policy approaches to strengthen the quality and impact of career guidance services in the Latin American countries under study remain limited and could be expanded for greater impact.

Co-ordinating all the stakeholders involved in career guidance is a challenge. Ministries of Labour or Education in collaboration with the public employment services are the public authorities most commonly responsible for adult career guidance in Latin America countries. Responsibilities are also split across central and regional levels of government. Very few mechanisms support co-ordination, and those that are in place mostly exclude important non-governmental stakeholders such as labour unions, employer groups and professional guidance associations.

The report begins with a summary of the main findings and policy recommendations.

1 Recommendations

Coverage and inclusiveness

Raise awareness about formal career guidance opportunities through media campaigns and active outreach to vulnerable groups

Many adults are not aware of career guidance services and rely strongly on informal sources of information, such as family and friends. This might be due to a lack of public information, and risks compounding inequalities in the labour market.

Provision and service delivery

Expand public provision (including PES) and associated funding to offer affordable or free high quality career guidance services to vulnerable adults

Vulnerable adults, such as the unemployed and low-educated adults, are less likely to use career guidance services in Latin America. Unequal access to services might be due to limited provision by public employment services.

Further expand the range of delivery channels available, and strengthen online career guidance platforms.

Face-to-face provision remains the most common channel of career guidance, while there is unmet demand for alternative channels such as instant messaging. Online career guidance platforms represent a cost-effective way to meet demand for professional career guidance. Existing platforms could be strengthened by providing personalised information based on skills assessments, by integrating information about job and training opportunities, and by giving users an opportunity to chat live with a counsellor directly on the platform.

Quality and impact

Strengthen general public service delivery quality standards and include a component that considers career guidance specifically

Competence frameworks for career guidance advisors are not yet in place and quality standards around service delivery are rare, with significant variation across local employment offices.

Develop a skills profiling tool that can be used by providers, particularly when working with adults who have no formal qualifications

Effective guidance relies on personalised assessments and recommendations about training and job pathways. Skills profiling tools can be extremely useful in contexts where adults lack formal qualifications, but they are not widely used in Latin America.

Governance and funding

Consider forming a working group with all relevant stakeholders to improve career guidance policy and provision

Stakeholders, such as social partners and professional guidance associations are often not part of the strategic governance of career guidance policy.

Develop a system of regular reporting standards between local employment offices, national ministries and other relevant public bodies, and facilitate international exchanges of good practice

Co-ordination mechanisms between the different levels of government and other public bodies responsible for career guidance exist, but could be strengthened. It may also be useful to organise regular exchanges of good practice and promising initiatives across Latin American countries.

Design financial measures to reduce the direct and indirect costs of career guidance for vulnerable adults

In Latin America, adults are more likely to pay out-of-pocket for career guidance than elsewhere. The cost of career guidance is a barrier, particularly for unemployed, informal and inactive workers.

2 Why is career guidance for adults important in Latin America?

A year after the outbreak of the COVID-19 pandemic, Latin American countries have experienced economic disruption and struggling labour markets. Even prior to the crisis, skills demand had been changing due to digitalisation, globalisation, population ageing and the transition to low-carbon economies. This chapter provides a brief overview of the labour market context in Latin America and suggests an increasingly important role for career guidance for adults.

In Brief

Latin American labour markets facing a number of challenges

The COVID-19 crisis has exacerbated existing challenges in Latin American labour markets, including high unemployment. The key findings of this chapter are outlined as follows:

- Latin American labour markets face a number of challenges. Unemployment is high relative to the OECD average, and there is a large share of workers in informal employment. High inequality translates to unequal educational outcomes, and educational attainment falls below the OECD average in the four Latin American countries studied. Despite poor performance on literacy and numeracy skills relative to the OECD average, adults in Latin American countries are also less likely to participate in training, which makes adults in these countries more vulnerable to the impacts of automation and associated changing skills demand.
- The impacts of the COVID-19 pandemic are likely to exacerbate these challenges. Unemployment rose in 2020, and the effects of the COVID-19 pandemic are likely to accelerate technological adoption going forward.
- Career guidance for adults is relatively rare in the Latin American context, though it could play an important role in supporting adults in finding new employment and adapting to changing skills demand. Career guidance is a set of services intended to assist individuals of all age groups to make well-informed educational, training, and occupational choices.

Introduction

The world of work is changing amid globalisation, technological change, population ageing and in response to environmental pressures. Previous OECD analyses have demonstrated that Latin American countries are also affected by these trends, although with some difference from other regions (OECD, 2020[1]). With a younger population and a slower speed of adoption of advanced technologies, Latin American countries have so far been somewhat sheltered from the impacts of population ageing and technological change. That said, the effects of the COVID-19 pandemic are likely to accelerate technological adoption going forward. Further, the sectoral composition of many Latin American countries – where extractive industries still play an important role – mean that policy efforts to reduce the impact of climate change may affect these countries more heavily.

In light of these changes, career guidance for adults represents a fundamental lever to help adults successfully navigate a constantly evolving labour market. In a recent cross-country review, the OECD defined career guidance as "a set of services that assist individuals in making well-informed educational, training and occupational choices" (OECD, 2021[2]). There is evidence from the literature of the positive impact of career guidance on learning outcomes, training participation, and, to a lesser extent, employment outcomes (OECD, 2004[3]; OECD, 2021[4]).

This report provides a comparative analysis of career guidance for adults in four Latin American countries: Argentina, Brazil, Chile and Mexico. It is based on a combination of desk research, video calls with stakeholders in each country, and policy questionnaire responses from Ministries of Labour and Education. The analysis also draws from the 2020 Survey of Career Guidance for Adults (SCGA). The SCGA is an online survey of adults' experience with career guidance. In a first phase of fieldwork, data was collected in Chile, Germany, France, Italy, New Zealand, and the United States, and in a second phase in Argentina, Brazil and Mexico. The report sometimes refers to 'Latin America' when discussing data collected for the four Latin American countries mentioned above to avoid repetition.

This report includes recommendations and five chapters. Chapter 2 describes the general skills and labour market context in Latin America. It then defines the concept of career guidance for adults, and how this concept is understood in Latin America. Chapter 3 presents findings on the coverage and inclusiveness of career guidance services based on the SCGA. Chapter 4 maps the career guidance provider landscape and presents data on the different channels of service delivery. Chapter 5 reviews existing evidence on the quality and impact of career guidance services, and discusses policy options to improve them in the future. Chapter 6 discusses the stakeholders and co-ordination mechanisms in place to govern career guidance systems as well as how costs for career guidance are shared among governments, employers and adults.

Labour market context in Latin America

Latin American countries have been hit hard by the COVID-19 crisis while facing continued structural challenges. Low productivity, high inequality and informality, combined with underfunded public services and institutions, complicate the responses to the pandemic and compromise the well-being of the population (OECD et al., 2020[5]). The demand and supply for labour and skills in Latin American labour markets have inevitably been affected by the crisis, as well as the ongoing global trends in digitalisation, globalisation, demographic change and the shift to a low-carbon economy.

Substantial underutilisation and underdevelopment of skills

Unemployment, underemployment and poor quality jobs all undermine the opportunities for adults to use and improve their skills and harm individual well-being and the productive potential of the economy. The impacts of the COVID-19 pandemic have increased unemployment in Latin American countries, where unemployment was already high prior to the pandemic. The average unemployment rate of the four Latin American countries rose from about 8% in 2019, to just over 10% in 2020 (Figure 2.1). This is about 3 percentage points above the OECD average. Working hours in the region also fell by 16% during 2020 (ILO; 2021[6]).

The labour under-utilisation rate is a broader measure than the unemployment rate. It measures the share of the labour force who are unemployed, marginally attached (i.e. persons not in the labour force but who wish to and are available to work), or underemployed (full-time workers working less than usual due to economic reasons or part-time workers who wanted to work full-time). Labour underutilisation is comparably high in Latin America and employment growth is expected to continue to decline (ILO, 2020[7]). Gender gaps also remain large in Latin American labour markets.

The share of young people (18-24 year-olds) neither employed nor in education or training ("NEET"), is an important indicator of the extent to which young people are not gaining additional skills either through on-the-job learning at work or through formal education and training. In 2019, it was above the OECD average (14%) in all four countries, and highest in Brazil (31%), followed by Argentina (24%), Mexico (22%) and Chile (22%) (OECD, 2020[8]).

Figure 2.1. Unemployment rate

Percentage of total labour force who are unemployed

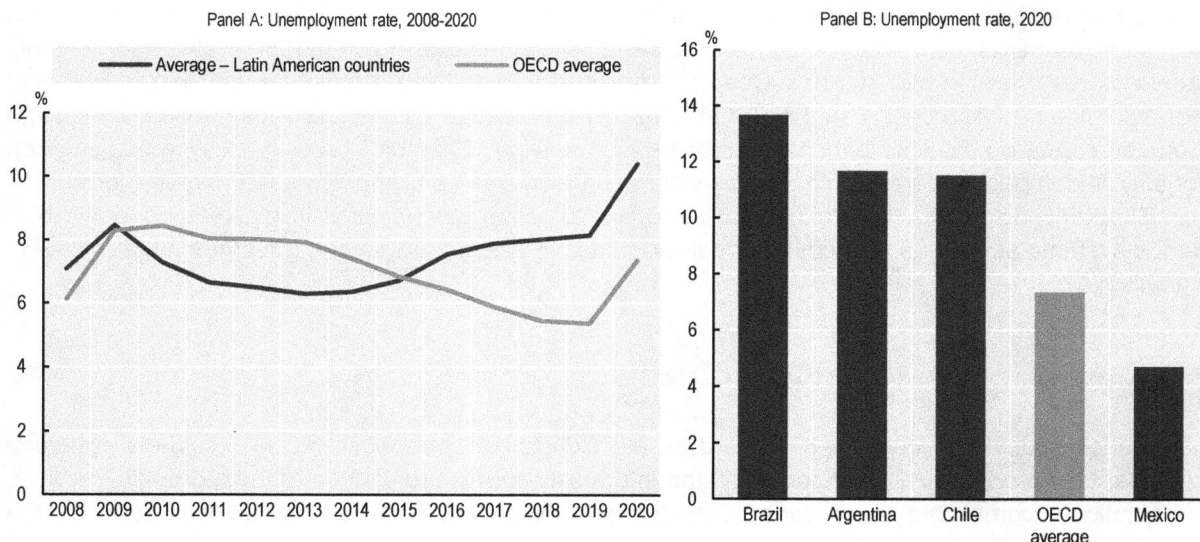

Panel A: Unemployment rate, 2008-2020

Panel B: Unemployment rate, 2020

Note: Panel A: Modelled ILO estimate, Average – Latin American countries includes Argentina, Brazil, Chile and Mexico.
Source: World Bank database https://data.worldbank.org/indicator/SL.UEM.TOTL.ZS?locations=ZJ, World Development Indicators.

In addition, Latin American labour markets are characterised by high informality, which may limit learning opportunities. Chile, Argentina, Brazil and Mexico have among the lowest shares of informal employment in Latin America, but the shares remain high (Figure 2.2). In Mexico, 46% of the adult population were employed in the informal sector in 2018 compared with 42% in Brazil and 40% in Argentina (CEDLAS and The World Bank, 2020[9]). The lowest share of informality is in Chile (32%). In comparison, undeclared work in the private sector in the EU is around 16%[1] (European Commission, 2017[10]). In all countries, informality is significantly higher in rural areas than in urban areas and higher for women than for men. High-educated workers are the least likely to work in informal employment.

As a result of the high rate of informal employment, job quality is relatively low in Latin American countries. Workers disproportionately work in low-productivity jobs that also pay comparatively low wages (ILO, 2020[7]). Earnings inequality is higher and workers in Latin America tend to be more vulnerable to labour market risks compared to OECD countries. In most emerging economies, this primarily reflects the risk of falling into very low pay. The quality of the working environment is also generally lower in Latin America, and one indication of this is the higher incidence of working very long hours (OECD, 2020[1]).

Figure 2.2. Informality

Percentage of adults (25-64) who are in informal employment (latest year available)

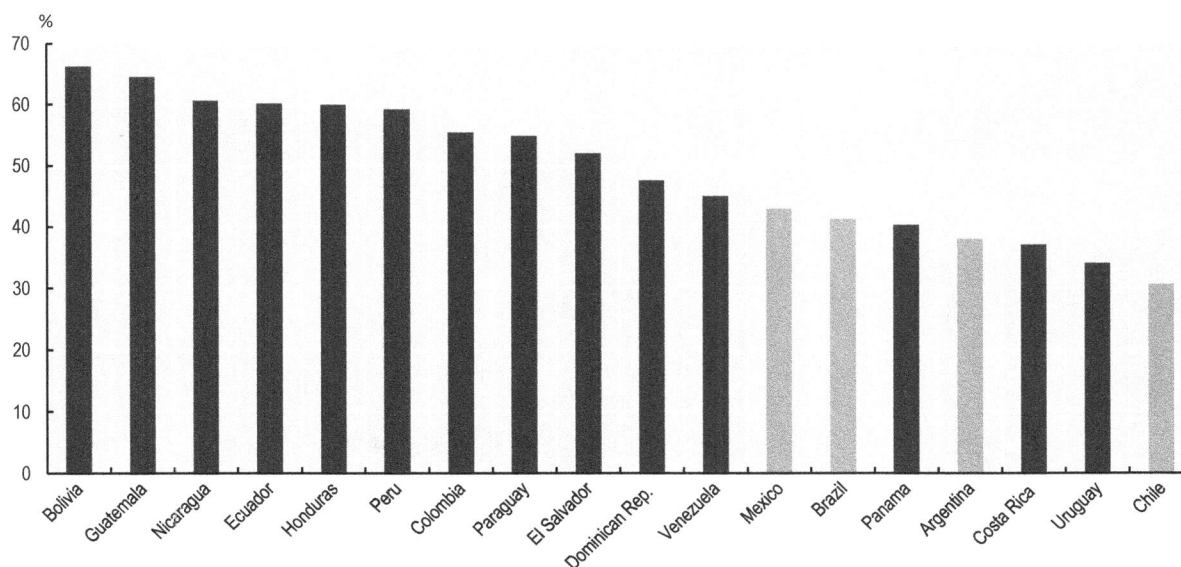

Source: SEDLAC (CEDLAS and The World Bank), Socio-Economic Database for Latin America and the Caribbean, http://www.cedlas.econo.unlp.edu.ar/wp/en/estadisticas/sedlac/.

Education and skills supply in Latin America

The Latin American region is one of the most unequal regions in the world (OECD, 2020[11]), which is reflected in unequal education outcomes, and means that a substantial portion of low-income adults are unable to afford training and career guidance. Using the Gini index, a statistical measure of economic inequality in a population on the scale of 0 (equal) to 1 (unequal), the region has an average Gini coefficient of 0.47, compared to an average of 0.31 in non-Latin American OECD countries. In 2018, Argentina recorded the lowest Gini coefficient (below 0.40), while Brazil recorded levels higher than 0.52. In both countries, inequality was higher in 2018 than in 2014. Chile's Gini coefficient remained stable at 0.45 in 2014 and 2018 and Mexico's latest data (2014) are similar, at 0.48.

While countries in Latin America have seen important improvements over the past years, educational attainment remains relatively low. On average, 56% of individuals aged 25-64 across Argentina, Brazil, Chile and Mexico have completed at least upper secondary education, compared with 79% on average across OECD countries. Chile has the highest share of adults who completed at least upper secondary education among the Latin American countries in this review (67%) (Figure 2.3). Argentina has the highest share with tertiary education (36%), a share close to the OECD average of 38%. A comparison to the educational attainment of the youngest adults (25-34) in this population shows a rising trend towards higher education: on average 69% of adults in this younger group have completed at least upper secondary education.

Figure 2.3. Educational attainment

Percentage of population (25-64 year-olds) having completed each level of education, 2019 or latest available year

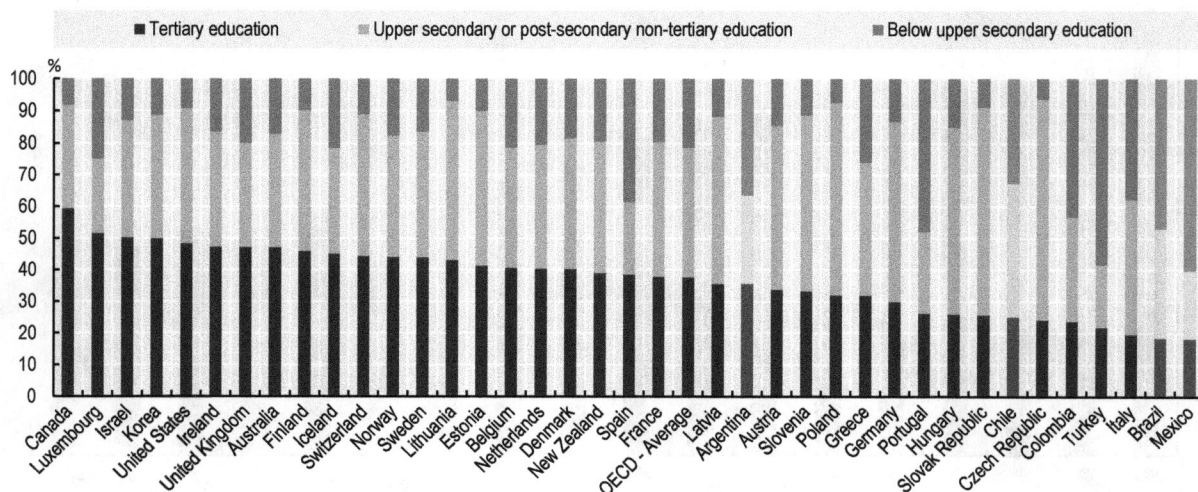

Source: OECD (2019), "Education at a Glance", OECD.Stat (database), http://stats.oecd.org.

More direct measures of skills also suggest that adult skills are relatively low in Latin American countries. In Chile and Mexico, the Latin American countries covered by the Survey of Adult Skills (PIAAC),[2] just over half of adults have low levels of literacy skills (53% and 51%, respectively) and an even higher share have low levels of numeracy skills (60% and 62%, respectively). For comparison, 20% of adults in the OECD on average have low literacy skills and less than 24% have low numeracy skills. This points to the need to boost lifelong learning, such as upskilling and reskilling opportunities for adults.

Despite the poor performance in terms of skill levels, participation in training is generally lower in Latin American countries than the OECD average. According to the PIAAC data, one out of three adults (30%) participate in formal or non-formal job-related training in the Latin American countries covered by the PIAAC survey, 10 percentage points below the OECD average of 40% (Figure 2.4). Approximately 57% of adults did not participate, and did not want to participate, in adult learning activities, compared to 49% in the OECD. However, levels of participation in adult learning in the region vary considerably, with Chile showing participation levels on par with the OECD average. Training intensity is also generally lower in Latin American countries, with a significantly smaller number of hours spent on non-formal job-related training per year than on average across OECD countries (OECD, 2020[1]).

Within Latin American countries, some groups participate in training less than others. Women participate significantly less in adult learning than men with a gap of 14 percentage points (pp) in Chile and 11 pp in Mexico. The gap in participation between low-wage and medium/high wage workers is even larger at 25 pp in Chile and 24 pp in Mexico. A sizeable gap is also found between workers with and without an employment contract, which strongly suggests that employment status and job quality are related to the take-up of training. Finally, a crucial factor influencing participation in training in Latin America is firm size: individuals working in micro and small firms (less than 250 employees) participate far less in training than those in larger firms with a gap of 27 pp in Chile and 32 pp in Mexico (OECD, 2020[1]).

Figure 2.4. Participation in adult learning

Percentage of adults who participated in formal or non-formal job-related adult learning in the past 12 months

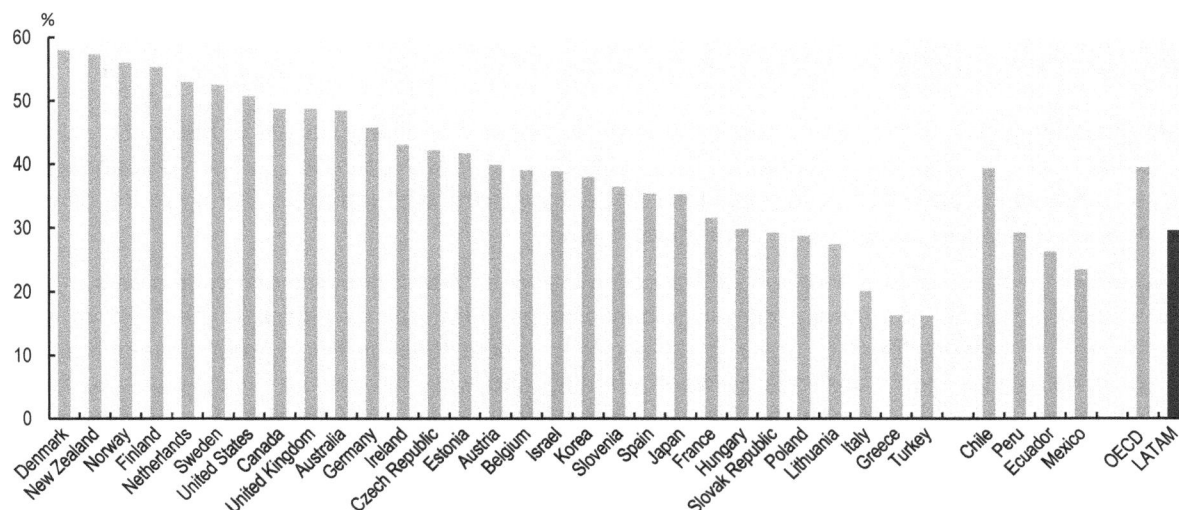

Note: LATAM refers to the average of the Latin American countries covered by the PIAAC survey, i.e. Chile, Ecuador, Mexico and Peru.
Source: OECD (2019), Dashboard on Priorities for Adult Learning, http://www.oecd.org/employment/skills-and-work/adult-learning/dashboard.htm.

Skills imbalances in Latin America

A range of indicators confirm larger gaps between labour market needs and workers' skills in Latin American countries, compared with the OECD average. Over-qualification, i.e. the share of workers whose education level is higher than that required by their job, is almost twice as high as the OECD average (17%), ranging from around 30% in Chile, Argentina and Brazil to 38% in Mexico. Under-qualification is also substantial in Argentina (21%) and Chile (17%), similar to in the OECD average (19%). In Brazil and Mexico this seems to be less of a concern, with only 9% and 13% of workers underqualified, respectively (OECD, 2017[12]).

In line with these imbalances, shortages of highly skilled professionals are relatively low in Argentina, Brazil, Chile and Mexico, as measured by employer surveys. Less than two out of ten jobs in shortage are high-skilled and the majority of jobs in demand are found, instead, in medium and to a lesser extent in low-skilled occupations. The highest demand for low-skilled employment among the four countries is found in Mexico (34%) and the highest demand for high-skilled labour is in Argentina (almost a third) (OECD, 2020[1]). Also, the share of firms that believe an inadequately educated workforce (either too high, too low or lacking the right set of skills) is a major constraint on their operations is high in the four countries, at more than half in Brazil (69% in 2012), 39% in Argentina (2017), 41% in Chile (2012) and 31% in Mexico (2012) (The World Bank, 2021[13]).

A major trend that is expected to further disrupt labour markets and amplify skills imbalances is automation. The adoption of digital and automation technologies is likely to accelerate in the future and will alter the world of work, as well as the skills needed for economies to thrive. Already the COVID-19 pandemic appears to be speeding up the use of digital technologies (McKinsey&Company, 2020[14]; The World Bank, 2017[15]; Reuters, 2020[16]). OECD estimates, using data from Chile, Ecuador, Mexico and Peru, suggest that an average of 24% of jobs in these countries face a high risk of automation, which is almost 10 percentage points higher than the OECD average of 15% (Nedelkoska and Quintini, 2018[17]). Across these Latin American countries, another 35% of jobs are estimated to experience significant changes in the tasks that workers carry out daily, a figure that is approximately 5 percentage points higher than the OECD average. Other studies find similar results (The World Bank, 2016[18]; Weller, Gontero and Campbell, 2019[19]; McKinsey Global Institute, 2017[20]).

Career guidance for adults in Latin America

Career guidance is a set of services intended to assist individuals of all age groups to make well-informed educational, training, and occupational choices (Box 2.1). In many countries, career guidance policy focuses on assisting young people to make their first entry into the labour market. But given the changing world of work, adults can benefit from career guidance too.

Quality career guidance entails an involved interaction that goes beyond quickly matching a person with a job or a training programme. Ideally, career guidance helps individuals to reflect on their strengths and interests, and empowers them to make good decisions about their lifelong career development and learning. It helps to bridge transitions between learning and work, by assisting individuals to identify promising career paths and to plot the necessary next steps in terms of training and development to achieve those career goals. In an ideal system, services offer individuals more than one-off encounters; instead, individuals meet more than once with a career guidance advisor who assists them before, during and after a career move or training decision.

Career guidance for adults, as conceived above, is relatively rare in the Latin American context. Dedicated career guidance activities directed at adults remain marginal and tend not to be set out as an explicit policy priority. Career guidance for adults is usually one component of a broader set of services, such as active labour market programmes, training programmes or labour intermediation services more generally.

While career guidance for adults has not received significant policy attention in Latin American countries, career guidance for youth has received more. Youth training programmes are widespread in the region, and mostly target disadvantaged young people. Often, these programs include a dedicated career guidance component.

The way that career guidance is conceived in Latin America has been influenced by factors such as the health of the labour market, pre-existing institutional structures, and their funding capacity. While labour intermediation services and active labour market policies have been strengthened considerably in the last decades, the Latin American region still lags behind other OECD countries in terms of public resources as well as institutional capacity for career guidance services. In addition, many Latin America countries do not have unemployment insurance and only very limited forms of income support for the unemployed. As a result of these resource constraints, the providers of labour intermediation services, and often individuals themselves, place a higher priority on matching individuals with jobs quickly, rather than supporting them in finding good long-term matches.

Strengthening career guidance for adults in Latin America has the potential to improve adults' career prospects and reduce inequality. An investment in personalised advice and guidance with a holistic perspective on the lifelong career development of individuals can assist them to make informed training and occupational choices. Career guidance helps align lifelong learning opportunities to both individual preferences and needs and labour market demand. This is especially important in the context of the COVID-19 pandemic as many adults need to upskill and retrain in a changed labour market. By improving the alignment of skills development with demand in the labour market, career guidance also empowers individuals, promotes social inclusion, and ultimately supports economic development through better skills matching.

Box 2.1. What is career guidance?

Career guidance, as defined in this report, refers to services to assist individuals of all age groups to make well-informed educational, training and occupational choices (OECD, 2021[4]; OECD, 2004[3]). Focussed on lifelong career development and learning, career guidance informs individuals about the labour market and education systems, and relates them to their own situation and available resources. It helps individuals to reflect on their strengths and abilities, as well as their qualifications and interests. Comprehensive career guidance provides assistance and advice to people to empower them to make good choices about lifelong career development and learning.

Across the globe, career guidance is known by different terms, including career development, career counselling, lifelong guidance, educational and vocational guidance and vocational psychology. In the Spanish-speaking Latin American countries, different terms are used: *orientación vocacional*, *orientación profesional*, *orientación laboral*, *orientación a lo largo de la vida desarrollo de carrera*.

Who delivers career guidance and how it is delivered vary. People offering career guidance can have training of different length and intensity. While face-to-face interviews are still a dominant channel, the provision of career guidance services has diversified in the last decades to include group discussions, printed information, advice via telephone or video call and online resources. Career guidance can be provided by educational institutions, public employment services, or companies. Services may be targeted to particular groups of adults, such as the unemployed or low-skilled, or may be open to anyone regardless of employment status.

Labour intermediation (*intermediación laboral*) is a related concept. The Inter-American Development Bank defined labour intermediation as "activities undertaken to improve the speed and quality of the match between available jobs, jobseekers and training. In this way, such services "intermediate" between labour supply and demand" (Mazza, 2003[21]). Labour intermediation may or may not entail speaking with a career guidance advisor or other career guidance components, such as skills assessments or training referral. As dedicated career guidance services are rare in the Latin American countries studied, this report also considers labour intermediation as a related concept that overlaps with career guidance.

References

CEDLAS and The World Bank (2020), *SEDLAC Statistics*, https://www.cedlas.econo.unlp.edu.ar/wp/en/estadisticas/sedlac/estadisticas/#1496165509975-36a05fb8-428b (accessed on 3 December 2020). [9]

European Commission (2017), *An evaluation of the scale of undeclared work in the European Union and its structural determinants*, https://op.europa.eu/en/publication-detail/-/publication/8c3086e9-04a7-11e8-b8f5-01aa75ed71a1/language-en (accessed on 27 January 2021). [10]

ILO (2021), *ILO Monitor. COVID-19 and the world of work. Seventh edition*, ILO Monitor, http://moz-extension://d0d98d2f-49ef-4138-9d5f-c5fd7a7ce929/enhanced-reader.html?openApp&pdf=https%3A%2F%2Fwww.ilo.org%2Fwcmsp5%2Fgroups%2Fpublic%2F---dgreports%2F---dcomm%2Fdocuments%2Fbriefingnote%2Fwcms_767028.pdf (accessed on 10 March 2021). [6]

ILO (2020), *World Employment and Social Outlook – Trends 2020*. [7]

Mazza, J. (2003), *Labor Intermediation Services: Considerations and Lessons for Latin America and the Caribbean from International Experience*, Inter-American Development Bank, https://publications.iadb.org/en/publication/11518/labor-intermediation-services-considerations-and-lessons-latin-america-and (accessed on 25 January 2021). [21]

McKinsey Global Institute (2017), *A future that works: Automation, employment and productivity*, http://moz-extension://b065121f-d7a2-4bbc-af7f-0e8bdc61c772/enhanced-reader.html?openApp&pdf=https%3A%2F%2Fwww.mckinsey.com%2F~%2Fmedia%2Fmckinsey%2Ffeatured%2520insights%2FDigital%2520Disruption%2FHarnessing%2520automation%2520for%2520a%2520future%2520that%2520works%2FMGI-A-future-that-works-Executive-summary.ashx (accessed on 7 December 2020). [20]

McKinsey&Company (2020), *How COVID-19 has pushed companies over the technology tipping point--and transformed business forever*, https://www.mckinsey.com/business-functions/strategy-and-corporate-finance/our-insights/how-covid-19-has-pushed-companies-over-the-technology-tipping-point-and-transformed-business-forever (accessed on 5 February 2021). [14]

Nedelkoska, L. and G. Quintini (2018), "Automation, skills use and training", *OECD Social, Employment and Migration Working Papers*, No. 202, OECD Publishing, Paris, https://dx.doi.org/10.1787/2e2f4eea-en. [17]

OECD (2021), *Career Guidance for Adults in a Changing World of Work*, OECD Publishing, Paris, https://www.oecd-ilibrary.org/employment/career-guidance-for-adults-in-a-changing-world-of-work_9a94bfad-en (accessed on 8 January 2021). [2]

OECD (2021), *Career Guidance for Adults in a Changing World of Work*, Getting Skills Right, OECD Publishing, Paris, https://dx.doi.org/10.1787/9a94bfad-en. [4]

OECD (2020), *Education at a Glance 2020: OECD Indicators*, OECD Publishing, Paris, https://dx.doi.org/10.1787/69096873-en. [8]

OECD (2020), *Effective Adult Learning Policies: Challenges and Solutions for Latin American Countries*, OECD Skills Studies, OECD Publishing, Paris, https://dx.doi.org/10.1787/f6b6a726-en. [1]

OECD (2020), *Latin American Economic Outlook - Digital Transformation for Building Back Better*, OECD, Paris, http://www.oecd.org/publications/latin-american-economic-outlook-20725140.htm (accessed on 1 December 2020). [11]

OECD (2017), *Getting Skills Right: Skills for Jobs Indicators*, Getting Skills Right, OECD Publishing, Paris, https://dx.doi.org/10.1787/9789264277878-en. [12]

OECD (2016), *OECD Employment Outlook 2016*, OECD Publishing, Paris, https://dx.doi.org/10.1787/empl_outlook-2016-en. [23]

OECD (2015), *Latin American Economic Outlook 2015: Education, Skills and Innovation for Development*, OECD Publishing, Paris, https://dx.doi.org/10.1787/leo-2015-en. [22]

OECD (2004), *Career Guidance and Public Policy. Bridging the Gap*, http://www.SourceOECD.org, (accessed on 25 January 2021). [3]

OECD et al. (2020), *Latin American Economic Outlook 2020: Digital Transformation for Building Back Better*, OECD Publishing, Paris, https://dx.doi.org/10.1787/e6e864fb-en. [5]

Reuters (2020), *Coronavirus accelerates European utilities' digital drive*, https://www.reuters.com/article/us-health-coronavirus-utilities-tech-foc-idUSKCN2560OK (accessed on 5 February 2021). [16]

The World Bank (2021), *Workforce / Percent of firms identifying an inadequately educated workforce as a major constraint - GovData360*, https://govdata360.worldbank.org/indicators/h8f847a5a?country=BRA&indicator=257&viz=bar_chart&years=2009 (accessed on 3 February 2021). [13]

The World Bank (2017), *How countries are using edtech (including online learning, radio, television, texting) to support access to remote learning during the COVID-19 pandemic*, https://www.worldbank.org/en/topic/edutech/brief/how-countries-are-using-edtech-to-support-remote-learning-during-the-covid-19-pandemic (accessed on 5 February 2021). [15]

The World Bank (2016), *World Development Report 2016: Digital Dividends*, https://www.worldbank.org/en/publication/wdr2016 (accessed on 7 December 2020). [18]

Weller, J., S. Gontero and S. Campbell (2019), *Cambio tecnológico y empleo: una perspectiva latinoamericana*, Cepal, http://www.cepal.org/apps (accessed on 7 December 2020). [19]

Notes

[1] As a percentage of total gross value added (GVA), 2013.

[2] Ecuador, Mexico, Chile and Peru.

3 Coverage and inclusiveness

A major challenge in most countries is to ensure that all adults have access to information and guidance to make informed career and training decisions. In Latin America, unemployed adults in particular use career guidance much less than those who are employed, despite having a greater need for support. This chapter presents survey findings on the use and inclusiveness of career guidance among adults in Latin America, the motivation for using career guidance, as well as the barriers to doing so. It describes the role of online career guidance platforms as well as more informal channels of career support, such as speaking with family and friends.

In Brief

Strengthening coverage and inclusiveness of career guidance in Latin America

Career guidance has the potential to reduce high labour market inequality in Latin America by ensuring that all adults, regardless of their socio-economic group, have access to good information and advice to make well-informed educational, training and occupational choices. The key findings of this chapter are outlined as follows:

- A substantial share of adults use career guidance services in the four Latin American countries covered by the SCGA. Some 42% of adults in these countries have spoken with a career guidance advisor over the last 5 years, and most of them had multiple interactions with advisors. On average across all countries where survey data is available, the coverage of career guidance services for adults was very similar (43%).

- However, the use of career guidance services is below average for many groups who already face disadvantages in the labour market and train less. A particularity that stands out across the four Latin American countries is the much lower use of career guidance services among unemployed adults (26% use career guidance) versus employed adults (48%), with a gap of 23 percentage points (pp). In non-Latin American countries covered by the SCGA, the divide between these two groups is almost non-existent. Important gaps in the four Latin American countries covered by this study also exist between high- and low-educated individuals (16 percentage points), prime-age (25-54) and older adults (over 54) (11 percentage point), as well as those in formal and informal employment (7 percentage points), with the latter groups using services less.

- The most common reasons to use career guidance services in Latin America are wanting to progress in one's current job (40%), needing help to choose a study/training opportunity (29%) and wanting to change jobs (23%). Compared to the overall average of all nine countries in the survey (28%), adults in Latin American countries are substantially less likely to report "looking for a job" as a reason (21%).

- Among adults who did not speak with a career guidance advisor over the past 5 years, 37% did not feel the need to, a share which is considerably lower than the average of all countries in the survey (50%). Another 33% of adults in Latin American countries reported not knowing these services existed. This percentage is higher than the average across all countries in the SCGA, which suggests a lack of information or availability of services in Latin American countries.

- A large share of adults in Latin American countries looked online for information on employment, education and training, ranging from 78% in Mexico to over 90% in Chile. This is higher than the overall average across all nine countries in the SCGA (73%). Most career guidance users looked online for information in addition to talking to a counsellor.

- Perhaps to compensate for a lack of formal career guidance opportunities, adults in Latin America are more likely to participate in informal career development opportunities (70% of adults versus 60% in all countries in the SCGA), like visiting a job fair or training provider. An important source of advice are family and friends, on whom at least 80% of adults in Chile, Argentina and Mexico rely "very much" or "to some degree", which is higher than the average of all countries in the SCGA.

Introduction

This chapter assesses the coverage and inclusiveness of career guidance in the four Latin American countries covered in this review: Argentina, Brazil, Chile and Mexico. Coverage is measured by the share of adults using career guidance services. Inclusiveness is measured by assessing how the use of career guidance varies according to socio-economic characteristics, employment status, contract type, sector and occupation.

Analysing the inclusiveness of career guidance systems is especially relevant in Latin America, where labour market inequalities are particularly high. Career guidance services that are offered at low or no cost for all adults can address inequalities by "levelling the playing field": ensuring that high-quality support and information on the labour market, training and job opportunities are available to all adults.

This chapter analyses online survey data on the participation and inclusiveness of career guidance services, the main reasons why adults typically seek career guidance in the first place in Latin America, the key barriers they face to the use of career guidance services and the use of online information as well as more informal career support.

What share of adults uses career guidance services in Latin America?

Some form of guidance services are available in each of the Latin American countries covered in this study. Career guidance is most often provided by private providers and privately paid, but the PES also offers services in each of the countries (see Chapter 4). A key question is whether existing services are accessible to all those who need them. To shed light on the coverage and inclusiveness of career guidance systems for adults, this report builds on the results of the 2020 OECD Survey of Career Guidance for Adults (SCGA), carried out in nine countries: Argentina, Brazil, Chile, France, Germany, Italy, Mexico, New Zealand and the United States (see survey methodology in Annex).

The use of career guidance is similar across all countries in the survey. According to the SCGA, 42% of adults have spoken with a career guidance advisor over the past five years on average across the Latin American countries covered in the survey – only 1 percentage point below the overall average (Figure 3.1). This means that the share of adults who use career guidance services in Latin American countries is very similar to the share in other countries in the SCGA. Adults in Argentina were most likely to speak with a career guidance advisor (43% of adults), while adults in Mexico were somewhat less likely to (41%).[1]

On average, adults in Latin American countries have more interactions with their advisors per year than the average across countries covered by the SCGA. The number of interactions between the adult and the advisor provides insights into whether there is continuity in the service delivery i.e. whether there is any follow-up after a first consultation. Most adults in Latin American countries who used career guidance services have multiple interactions with advisors (79% of adults). Figure 3.2 shows that only one in six adults (21%) who spoke with a career guidance advisor over the past year had a single interaction; 32% had two interactions, 23% had three interactions and 24% spoke with a career guidance advisor more than three times.

Figure 3.1. Use of career guidance services among adults

Percentage of adults who have spoken with a career guidance advisor over the past 5 years

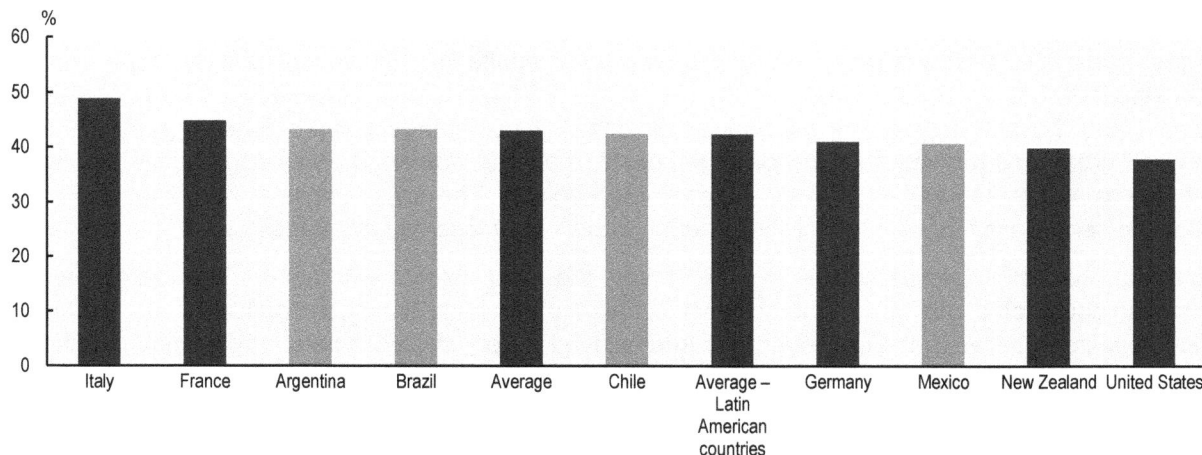

Note: Average – Latin American countries includes Argentina, Brazil, Chile and Mexico. Average includes Argentina, Brazil, Chile, France, Germany, Italy, Mexico, New Zealand and the United States.
Source: OECD 2020 Survey of Career Guidance for Adults (SCGA).

Figure 3.2. Intensity of use of career guidance services among adults

Percentage of adults who spoke with a career guidance advisor over the past year, by number of interactions

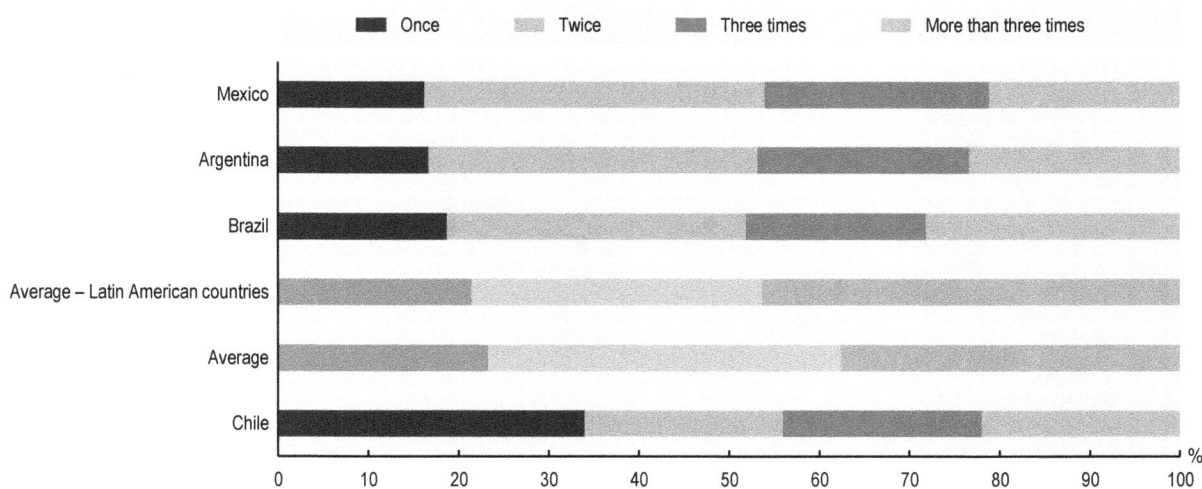

Note: Average – Latin American countries includes Argentina, Brazil, Chile and Mexico. Average includes Argentina, Brazil, Chile, France, Germany, Italy, Mexico, New Zealand and the United States.
Source: OECD 2020 Survey of Career Guidance for Adults (SCGA).

Is adult career guidance in Latin American countries inclusive?

Inclusive career guidance systems are accessible to everybody and especially reach disadvantaged groups who are most in need of advice about labour market and training options. This includes unemployed people, adults with low levels of education, migrants with foreign qualifications, or older individuals with outdated skills.

Based on the results of the SCGA, Figure 3.3 shows the differences in the use of career guidance services by socio-economic and demographic groups in the Latin American countries covered by the survey. The largest gaps exist between employed and unemployed adults (23 percentage points), high- and low-educated individuals (16 percentage points), prime-age (25-54) and older adults (over 54) (11 percentage points), and those in formal and informal employment (7 percentage points). Smaller gaps are found between urban and rural areas (3 percentage points), men and women (3 percentage points), as well as permanent and temporary employees (3 percentage points). The data indicates that access to career guidance services is more limited for those adults who already face disadvantages on the labour market.

Compared with all countries covered by the survey, the most notable difference in the results for Latin American countries concerns the unemployed. Across the four Latin American countries in the survey, the gap in coverage between the employed and unemployed is very large (23 percentage points), compared to a much smaller gap across all nine countries in the survey (10 percentage points). In non-Latin American countries in the survey, unemployed adults use career guidance as much as employed adults, with no gap between the two groups. The data suggests that access to career guidance services for unemployed adults might be particularly limited in Latin American countries.

There are other notable differences: the gap in the use of career guidance services between high-educated and low-educated adults is slightly higher in Latin American compared with other countries covered by the SCGA. In contrast, the gap between adults in urban and rural areas, between men and women as well as permanent and temporary employees on average is slightly smaller in Latin American countries than other countries in the survey.

Figure 3.3. Use of career guidance services, by socio-economic and demographic characteristics

Percentage of adults who have spoken with a career guidance advisor over the past 5 years, by groups

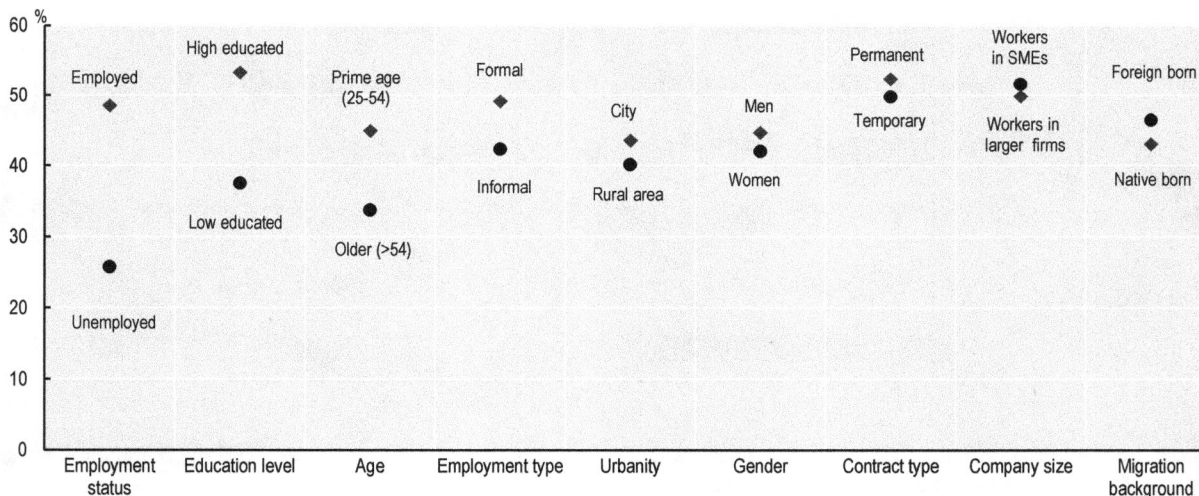

Note: Average of Argentina, Brazil, Chile and Mexico. The sample size of living in rural area is smaller than 50 observations in all four countries. The low educated group includes adults with a low or medium level of education (i.e. less than a bachelor's degree).
Source: OECD 2020 Survey of Career Guidance for Adults (SCGA).

The use of career guidance services also varies by occupation, with people working in low-skilled occupations using career guidance services less than those in high-skilled occupations (Figure 3.4) On average across the four Latin American countries, the use of career guidance is lowest among adults in less-skilled occupations (e.g. elementary occupations,[2] craft and related trade workers): in these jobs, just over 30% of adults have spoken to a career guidance advisor over the past five years. These also tend to be the occupations with a relatively higher risk of automation, according to OECD analysis (Nedelkoska and Quintini, 2018[1]). The use of career guidance services is highest among more skilled occupations, such as managers, technicians, professionals or skilled agricultural workers, where the share is 50% or more. This pattern is very similar across OECD countries with available data.

Figure 3.4. Use of career guidance services among adults, by occupation

Percentage of people who spoke with a career guidance advisor over the past 5 years, by occupation

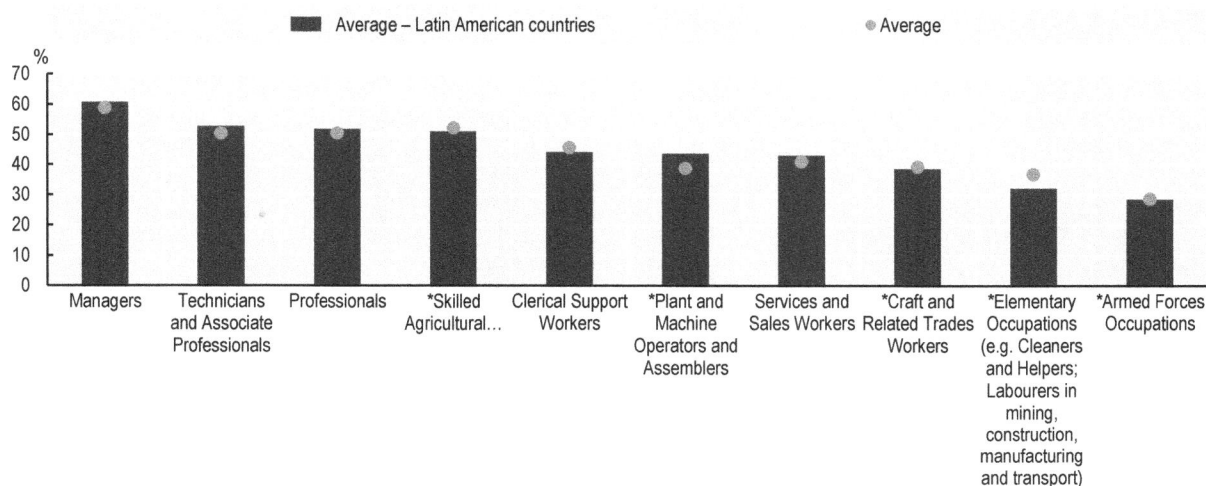

Note: Average – Latin American countries includes Argentina, Brazil, Chile and Mexico. Average includes Argentina, Brazil, Chile, France, Germany, Italy, Mexico, New Zealand and the United States. Elementary occupations include: cleaners and helpers; labourers in mining, construction, manufacturing and transport. Professionals include: science and engineering professionals, health professionals, teaching professionals, business and administration professionals, information and communications technology professionals, legal, social and cultural professionals. The sample sizes of starred occupations are smaller than 50 in these 9 countries.
Source: OECD 2020 Survey of Career Guidance for Adults (SCGA).

Why do adults seek career guidance in Latin America?

Adults in Latin America pursue career guidance for slightly different reasons than adults in other countries. The most common reasons are wanting to progress in one's current job (40%), needing help to choose a study/training opportunity (29%) and wanting to change jobs (23%) (Figure 3.5). Compared with the overall average of countries in the survey, adults in Latin American countries are less likely to report "looking for a job" as the reason for seeking career guidance (21% versus 28%). This may reflect fewer opportunities for career guidance provided by the public employment service in Latin American countries, or less generous unemployment insurance. Jobseekers without generous unemployment insurance are under higher pressure to find a job quickly to be able to support themselves and their families, which might reduce the likelihood that they take the time to use career guidance services when looking for a job. Uncertainty about future prospects or being required to speak with a career guidance advisor were the least common reasons reported (13% and 12% of adults, respectively).

While uncertainty about future prospects was not a common reason for speaking with a career guidance advisor, adults who are more worried about their labour market prospects are more likely to seek career guidance. This is the case on average across the nine countries in the survey, but the pattern is substantially more pronounced in Latin American countries (Figure 3.6). Adults who are more negative about their labour market prospects were much more likely to speak with a career guidance advisor. Confidence about one's future labour market prospects is a crucial indicator for whether a person speaks to a career guidance advisor in Latin America.

Figure 3.5. Reasons for speaking with a career guidance advisor

Percentage of adults who spoke with a career guidance advisor over the past 5 years, by reason

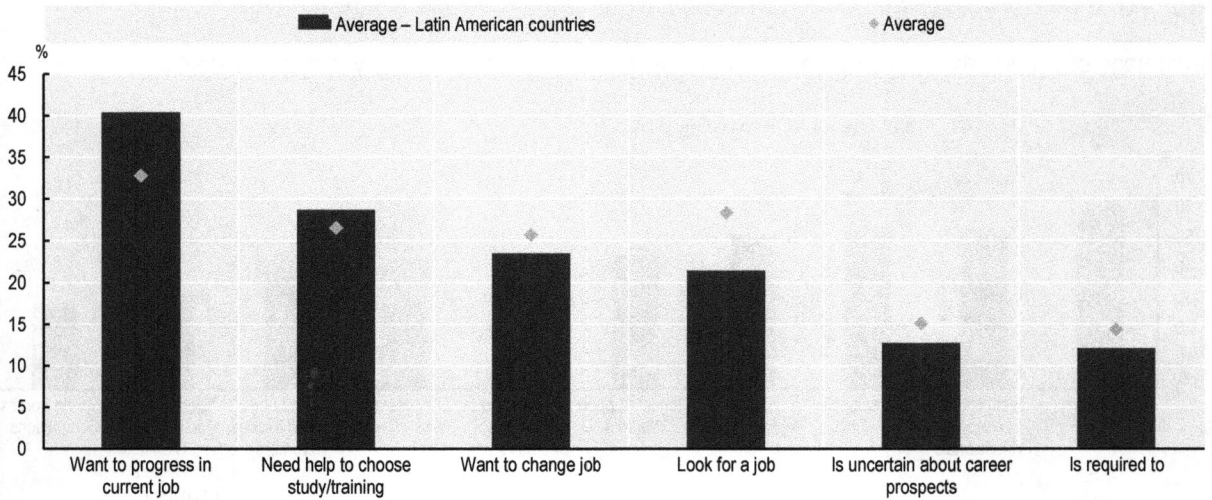

Note: Average – Latin American countries includes Argentina, Brazil, Chile and Mexico. Average includes Argentina, Brazil, Chile, France, Germany, Italy, Mexico, New Zealand and the United States. Respondents could choose more than one answer. Data refers to the last time the respondent spoke to a career guidance advisor.
Source: OECD 2020 Survey of Career Guidance for Adults (SCGA).

Figure 3.6. Use of career guidance services among adults by level of confidence in future labour market prospects

Percentage of adults who spoke with a career guidance advisor (in the past 5 years), by level of confidence about future labour market prospects

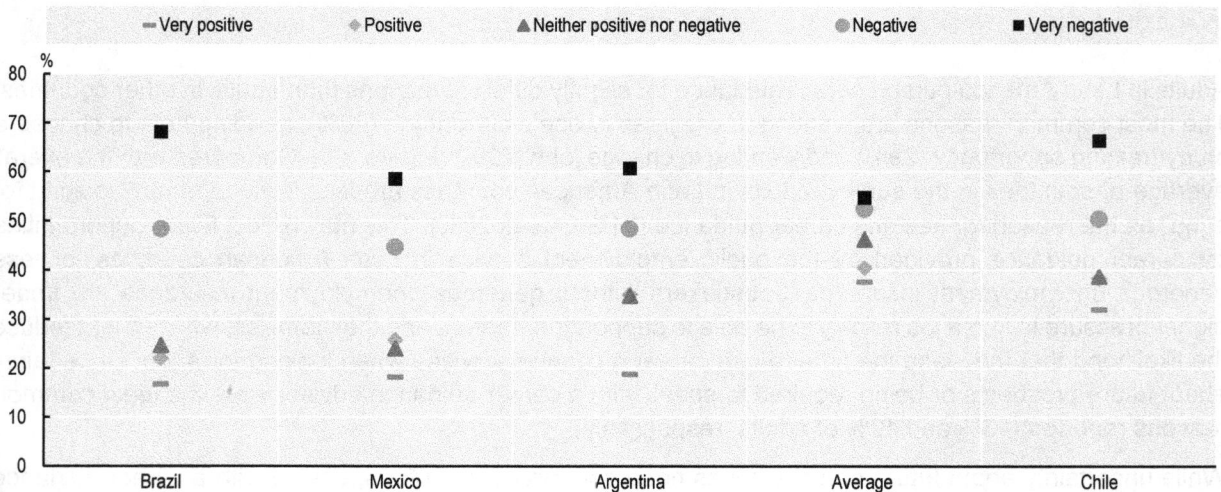

Note: Average includes Argentina, Brazil, Chile, France, Germany, Italy, Mexico, New Zealand and the United States.
Source: OECD 2020 Survey of Career Guidance for Adults (SCGA).

What are the barriers to accessing career guidance in Latin America?

To make career guidance systems more inclusive, it is important to understand the barriers adults face in accessing these services. Among adults who did not speak with a career guidance advisor over the past 5 years, 37% did not feel the need to (Figure 3.7). These adults may already be established in their careers, not planning a change in their working lives or not interested in education and training opportunities. Another explanation is that they are not fully aware of or informed about the benefits of receiving professional career guidance. This share of adults is relatively low, however, compared to the average of all nine countries in the survey, where 50% of respondents did not feel the need to talk with a career guidance advisor.

About 40% of adults did not speak to a career guidance advisor either because they did not know such services existed (33%) or they did not find one (7%). Both of these shares are higher than the overall average (24% and 4%, respectively). The data suggests that there is a lack of information about career guidance services and more efforts are needed to advertise them more comprehensively in Latin America. It is also possible that adults are not aware of career guidance services because these services are not available nationwide or do not sufficiently cover all social groups.

8% of adults reported that career guidance services are too costly, which is considerably above the SCGA average (5%). This suggests that introducing financial incentives to use career guidance services might have a bigger impact in Latin America than elsewhere. Other reasons why adults did not speak with a career guidance advisor over the past 5 years were that they did not have time, either due to work obligations, or family and childcare responsibilities (7% and 5%, respectively). The remaining adults did not do so because career guidance services were delivered at an inconvenient time or place (2%), or because of the poor quality of career guidance advisors (1%).

Figure 3.7. Reasons for not speaking with a career guidance advisor

Percentage of adults who did not speak with a career guidance advisor over the past 5 years by reason

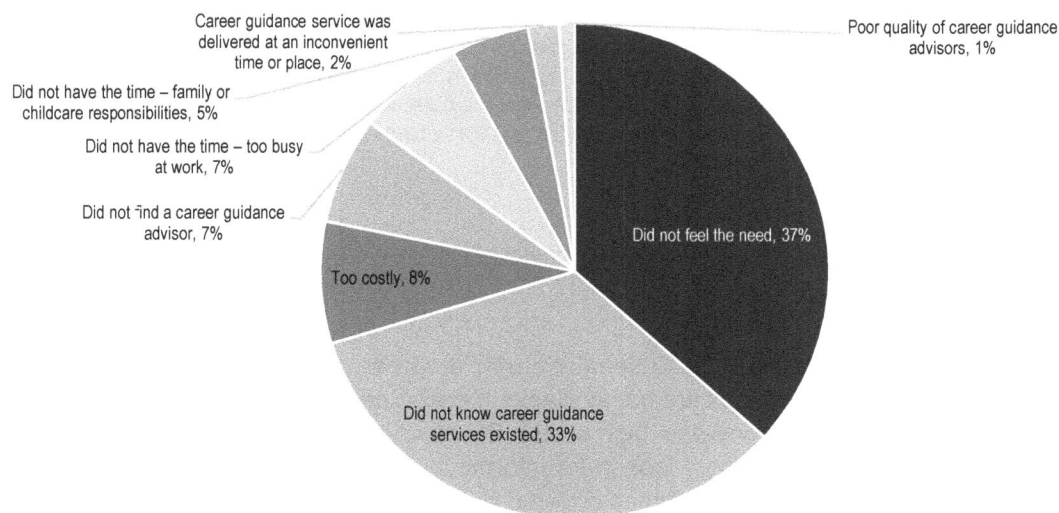

Note: Average of Argentina, Brazil, Chile and Mexico.
Source: OECD 2020 Survey of Career Guidance for Adults (SCGA).

In Latin America, informal workers, low-educated adults, and the unemployed tend to report not needing career guidance less than their more advantaged counterparts. These groups are likely aware of their greater vulnerability in the labour market, in terms of higher risk of job automation, lower job security and a lower likelihood of participating in training. However, of those adults who did not feel the need for career guidance, some are part of groups who would potentially benefit from career guidance services. In particular, 52% of older adults and 44% of temporary workers said that they did not feel the need to speak to a career guidance advisor – shares that are higher than among younger cohorts and permanent workers (Figure 3.8). Men and women as well as foreign and native-born adults were equally likely to respond that they did not feel the need for guidance (37%).

Figure 3.8. Not feeling a need to speak with a career guidance advisor by socio-economic and demographic characteristics

Percentage of adults who looked online for information on employment, education and training opportunities over the past 5 years, by group

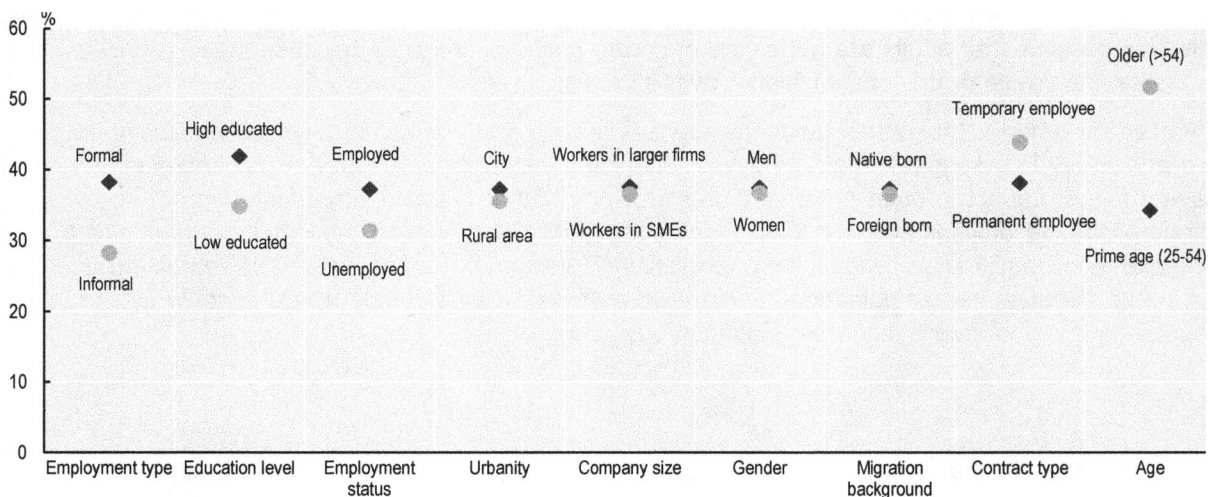

Note: Average of Argentina, Brazil, Chile and Mexico. The sample size of living in rural area is smaller than 50 observations in all four countries. The sample size of foreign-born is smaller than 50 observations in all four countries. The sample size of temporary contract is smaller than 50 observations in all four countries. The sample size of informal employment is smaller than 50 observations in all four countries. The low educated group includes adults with a low or medium level of education (i.e. less than a bachelor's degree).
Source: OECD 2020 Survey of Career Guidance for Adults (SCGA).

What share of adults look online for information on employment and training options in Latin America?

Online information is a good complement to speaking with a career guidance advisor and a possible alternative where such guidance services are not available. It is also not affected by several of the barriers mentioned above (inconvenient time or place, high costs). Based on the SCGA, 84% of adults in the Latin American countries covered by the survey looked for information online over the past 5 years, which is higher than the average across all nine countries covered by the SCGA. Mexico had the lowest share of adults looking for information online (78% of adults) and Chile had the highest share at over 90% (Figure 3.9). These high numbers may be due to relatively high access to internet in this region.[3] However, they could also be due to limited availability of subsidised opportunities to speak with a career guidance advisor (see Chapter 4).

Survey evidence suggests that online information complements rather than replaces speaking to a career guidance advisor. Among the 43% of adults who spoke with a career guidance advisor, nearly all (93%)

also looked for information online; 40% of adults both looked for information online and spoke with a career guidance advisor (see Figure 3.10).

Figure 3.9. Use of online information

Percentage of adults who looked online for information on employment, education and training opportunities over the past 5 years

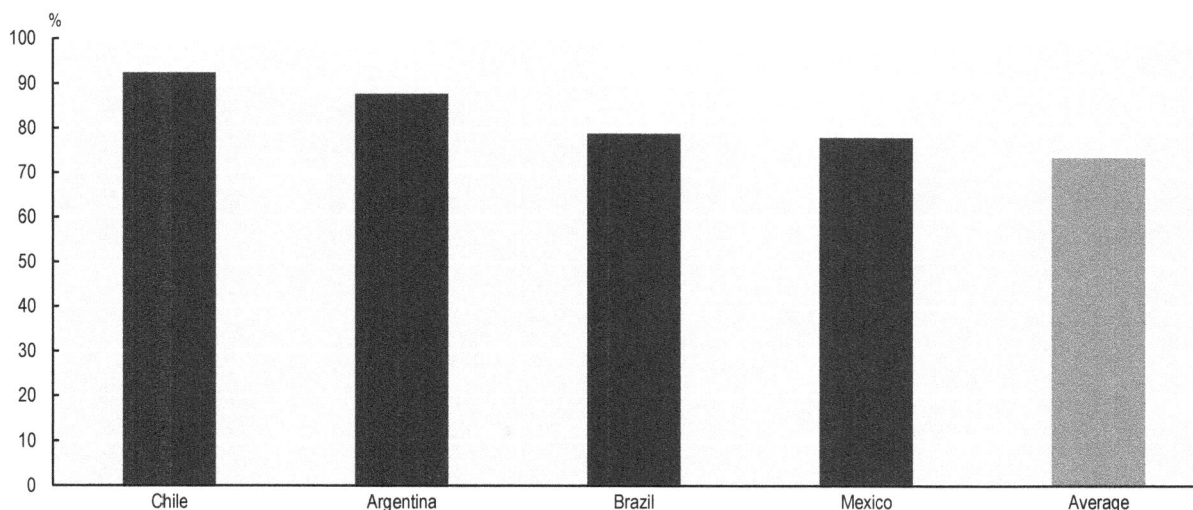

Note: Average includes Argentina, Brazil, Chile, France, Germany, Italy, Mexico, New Zealand and the United States.
Source: OECD 2020 Survey of Career Guidance for Adults (SCGA).

Figure 3.10. Use of career guidance and online information

Percentage of adults who spoke with a career guidance advisor and / or looked online for information on employment, education and training opportunities over the past 5 years

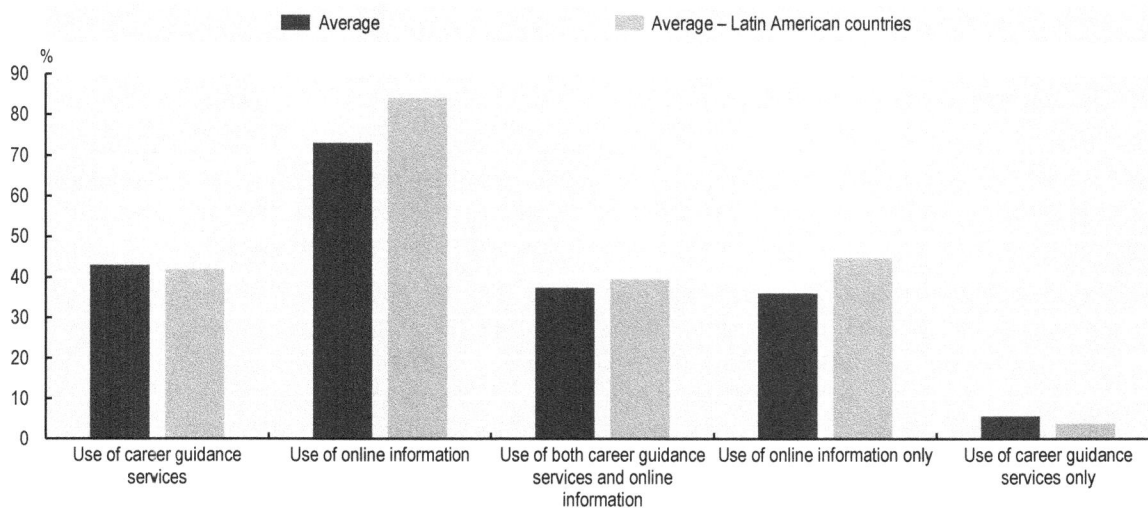

Note: Average includes Argentina, Brazil, Chile, France, Germany, Italy, Mexico, New Zealand and the United States. Average – Latin American countries includes Argentina, Brazil, Chile and Mexico.
Source: OECD 2020 Survey of Career Guidance for Adults (SCGA).

Some adults are less likely to look online for information about education and employment opportunities (Figure 3.11). The largest gaps in looking for information online are found between prime-age (25-54) and older (over 54) adults (13 percentage points), followed by high- and low-educated adults (9 percentage point). Older and lower-educated adults may feel less comfortable initiating their own online information searches, or may not have the necessary digital skills. In contrast, adults in informal employment look for information online more often than those in formal employment (5 percentage points), perhaps to compensate for having fewer opportunities to speak with a career guidance advisor than workers in formal employment. Gaps between the different groups using information online are less pronounced compared to speaking to a career guidance advisor, which suggests that access to online information is more inclusive.

Figure 3.11. Use of online information, by socio-economic and demographic characteristics

Percentage of adults who looked online for information on employment, education and training opportunities over the past 5 years, by group

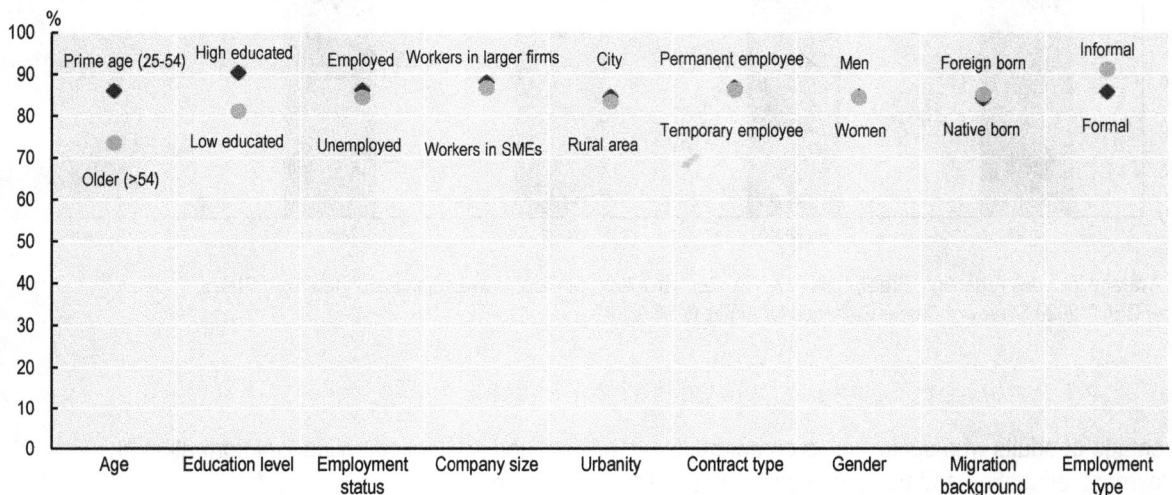

Note: Average of Argentina, Brazil, Chile and Mexico. The sample size of living in rural area is smaller than 50 observations in all four countries. The low educated group includes adults with a low or medium level of education (i.e. less than a bachelor's degree).
Source: OECD 2020 Survey of Career Guidance for Adults (SCGA).

Adults look online for information on employment, education and training opportunities for various reasons. The highest share of adults who look for information online are looking for information on education and training programmes. Figure 3.12 highlights the main types of information that adults look for online:

- The most common type of information that adults look for online is information about available education and training programmes (46% of adults who look online). About a third of all respondents are interested to learn more about the cost of education and training programmes (31%). Fewer adults look for financial support available to meet training costs (14%) and for information on the quality of training providers (13%). Finding information about the quality of training providers was a lower priority among adults in Latin American countries (13%) compared with non-Latin American countries (18%), where use of quality labels is more widespread than in the Latin American countries.

- More than a third of adults (36%) looked for information on how to search/apply for a job.

- A quarter of adults (26%) look online to understand how to have their skills and competences certified or assessed (e.g. through recognition of prior learning processes).
- Some adults go online to find out about jobs in demand (or those forecasted to be in demand) (27 and 18%, respectively, in Latin American and non-Latin American countries).

Figure 3.12. Type of information sought online

Percentage of adults who looked online for information on employment, education and training opportunities over the past 5 years, by type of information sought

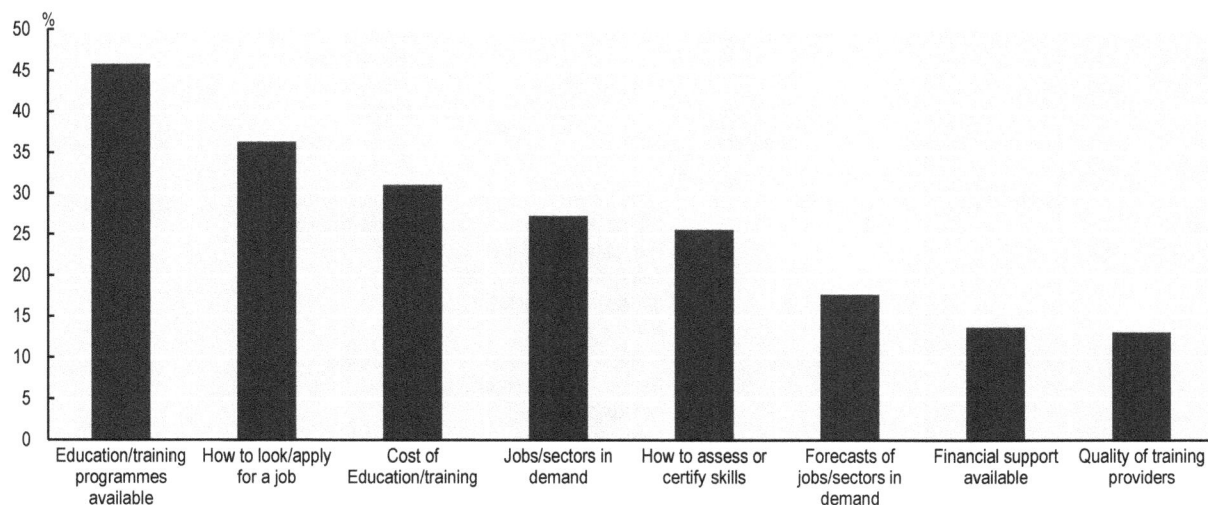

Note: Average of Argentina, Brazil, Chile and Mexico.
Source: OECD 2020 Survey of Career Guidance for Adults (SCGA).

The offer of online sources for information on employment, education and training opportunities varies greatly among the four countries (Table 3.1). Most public career guidance and labour intermediation platforms focus on one aspect of guidance such as posting vacancies or training options, compiling labour market information or support with administrative procedures. Many platforms offer users to create an account and facilitate follow-up over the job search process, e.g. Emprega Brasil, Chile's Bolsa Nacional de Empleo and Mexico's Portal del Empleo. Most websites that include a job portal, have a dedicated interface for potential employees and one for employers. Some of the websites enable direct interaction with a career guidance advisor by telephone or chat, such as Mexico's Portal del Empleo or ChileValora. The *Observatorio laboral* website in Mexico is a good practice example of a one-stop shop offering personalised guidance about job vacancies and training opportunities based on a skills assessment (Box 3.1).

Table 3.1. Public career guidance and labour intermediation platforms

Country	Platform name	Platform name in English	Provider	Content	URL
Argentina	El camino hacia tu próximo empleo	The path to your next job	Central government	Job search advice	www.argentina.gob.ar/trabajo/preparate
	Portal de Capacitación	Training portal	INAP (Instituto Nacional de la Administración Pública, INAP)	Training courses	https://capacitacion.inap.gob.ar
Brazil	Trabalha Brasil	Work Brazil	SINE	Job portal, labour market information	www.trabalhabrasil.com.br

Country	Platform name	Platform name in English	Provider	Content	URL
	Emprega Brasil	Employ Brazil	Labour Ministry	Job portal, job search advice, administrative information	https://empregabrasil.mte.gov.br
	Escola do Trabalhador	Worker's School	Ministry of Economy	Training courses	http://escola.trabalho.gov.br
Chile	Bolsa Nacional de Empleo	National Job Portal	Bolsa Nacional de Empleo	Job portal	www.bne.cl
	Orientación Laboral	Labour orientation	SENCE	Job search advice, personal online career guidance	https://sence.gob.cl/personas/orientacion-laboral
	Apoyo al Empleo	Employment support	SENCE	Job search advice, administrative information, training courses	https://apoyoalempleo.cl
	Observatorio Laboral	Labour Observatory	SENCE	Labour market information	https://observatorionacional.cl
	Destino Empleo	Destination Employment	ChileValora, Ministry of Labour and Social Protection, Fundación Telefónica Movistar, Inter-american Development Bank	Job portal, labour market information	www.destinoempleo.cl
	ChileValora	Chile values	Comisión del Sistema Nacional de Certificación de Competencias Laborales	Information on the certification of skills	www.chilevalora.cl
Mexico	Portal del Empleo	Employment Portal	SNE, Secretaria del Trabajo y Previsión Social	Job portal, administrative information, information about training opportunities	www.empleo.gob.mx
	Observatorio laboral	Labour Observatory	Secretaría del Trabajo y Previsión Social, SNE	Job search advice, labour market information	www.observatoriolaboral.gob.mx
	Programa de capacitación a distancia para trabajadores (Procradist)	Distance training programme for workers	Secretaria del Trabajo y Previsión Social	Training courses	www.procadist.gob.mx/portal/

Box 3.1. The labour observatory in Mexico

The Secretariat of Labor and Social Welfare, through the National Employment Service (STPS and SNE, for their acronym in Spanish) runs the dedicated career guidance platform *Observatorio Laboral*. The platform serves as a one-stop shop, connecting a range of guidance tools, relying on different sources of information and data, as well as using automated processes for interactive guidance experiences.

The guidance tools include:

- A vocational test composed of 40 questions about the user's skills and preferences. After completing the test, the website suggests training programmes and job profiles that match the provided information on the user.

- A section where the users can look up detailed descriptions of the training and/or job profiles that have been suggested to them.

- A vacancy database that can be sorted by indicators of the user's interest, e.g. the jobs with the highest salaries, those most demanded by young people, careers with the highest participation of women, as well as a training database with direct links to the training offer, including specific upskilling and reskilling opportunities for adults.

- An automated tool that compares two career options, e.g. in terms of salary or gender ratio.

- Videos of workers presenting their jobs and what job seekers can expect from choosing that profession, as well as videos presenting study programmes, not only what is taught, but also what that knowledge is used for in the labour market.

- A detailed guideline on how to write CVs and application letters, how to prepare for an interview, access to educational and labour market publications and guidance on how to become self-employed.

The website uses data collected by the Ministry of Education in Mexico (Secretaría de Educación Pública, SEP) on enrollment and graduation at the level of professional education, and other resources such as the National Occupation and Labour Survey (*Encuesta Nacional de Ocupación y Empleo, ENOE*), the National Occupational Classification System (*Sistema Nacional de Clasificación de Ocupaciones, SINCO*) and the information of the Mexican Classification of Study Programs by Fields of Academic Training (CMPE, by its Spanish acronym). While the design and language is rather directed at a younger target group, its offer is just as useful for all adults.

Source: Gobierno de México (n.d.[2]). *Observatorio Laboral*, www.observatoriolaboral.gob.mx/#/ (accessed on 4 March 2021).

Adults who did not look for information online (only 27% of adults in Latin American countries), reported similar barriers as for not using career guidance more generally (Figure 3.13). These included: not needing the information (47%), not having the time to do so for work-related or family related reasons (15% and 10%, respectively) or a lack of awareness about the availability of information online (15%). Not having internet access or computer skills were very minor barriers (6% and 4%, respectively). This will partly reflect that adults completing the online survey were more likely than those in the overall population to have internet access and digital skills.

Figure 3.13. Reasons for not looking online

Percentage of adults who did not look online for information on employment, education and training opportunities over the past 5 years, by reason

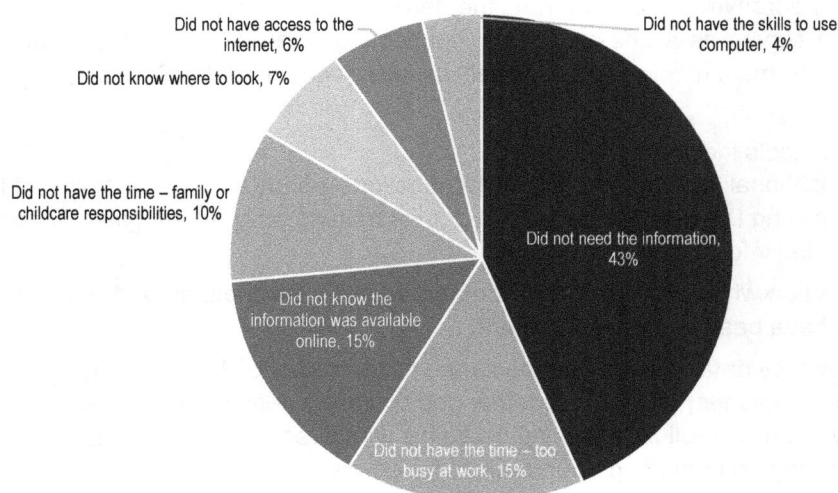

Note: Average of Argentina, Brazil, Chile and Mexico.
Source: OECD 2020 Survey of Career Guidance for Adults (SCGA).

Informal means to access information about employment, education and training opportunities

Adults in Latin American countries tend to rely more heavily on the advice of family and friends when making career and training decisions. At least 80% of adults in Chile, Argentina and Mexico rely "very much" or "to some degree" on the advice of family and friends to make choices that will affect working life (Figure 3.14). This is higher than the average observed across the nine countries covered by the SCGA (71%). Brazil is closer to the average (69% of adults). Higher reliance on family and friends may reflect strong social networks in these countries. It could also reflect that adults in Chile, Argentina and Mexico have fewer opportunities to access subsidised formal career support (see Chapter 4). Such reliance on family and friends for information could compound inequalities in the labour market, as highly educated adults or those from more privileged socio-economic backgrounds tend to have networks of family and friends who are better informed and better connected.

Adults in Latin American countries are also more likely to participate in informal career development activities than adults in other countries (Figure 3.15). Examples of career development activities include speaking with a human resource professional or a manager at work, visiting a job fair, visiting a training provider, participating in a job rotation/work site visit, or doing an internship. About 70% of adults in Latin American countries participated in at least one of these activities, which is above the 60% average across all nine countries in the SCGA. Again, this could point to fewer subsidised formal career guidance opportunities in Latin American countries. The most common activities were visiting a job fair (21%) and visiting a training provider (15%). Career development activities that take place within a worker's company (e.g. job rotation, internship, discussing performance with manager or HR professional) were least common, with fewer than 15% of adults participating in each of these activities.

Figure 3.14. Reliance on the advice of family and friends to make choices that will affect working life

Percentage all adults, by level of reliance

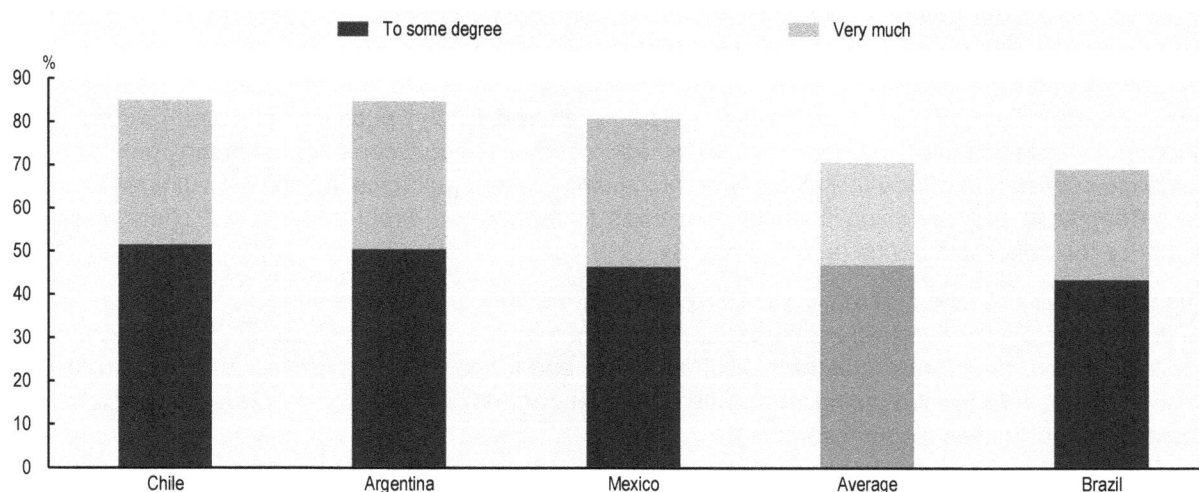

Note: Average includes Argentina, Brazil, Chile, France, Germany, Italy, Mexico, New Zealand and the United States.
Source: OECD 2020 Survey of Career Guidance for Adults (SCGA).

Figure 3.15. Participation in career development activities

Percentage of adults who participated in other types of career development activities over the past year, by activity

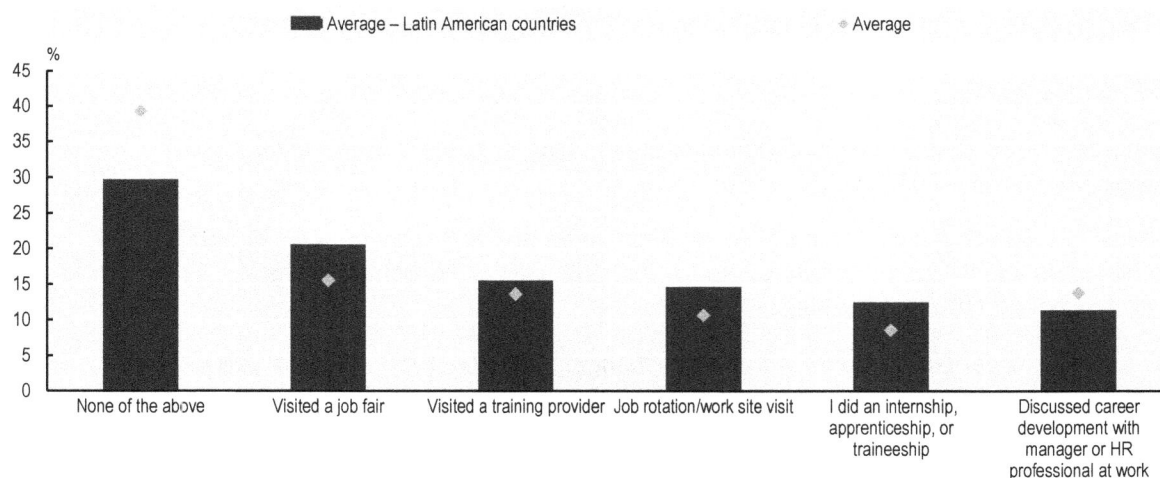

Note: Average – Latin American countries includes Argentina, Brazil, Chile and Mexico. Average includes Argentina, Brazil, Chile, France, Germany, Italy, Mexico, New Zealand and the United States. Respondents could choose more than one answer. Data refers to the last time the respondent spoke to a career guidance advisor.
Source: OECD 2020 Survey of Career Guidance for Adults (SCGA).

Recommendations

Low-educated adults, unemployed and older adults are less likely to use career guidance than their counterparts in Latin America. Unemployed adults in particular use career guidance services much less than employed adults in Latin America, while there is almost no gap in coverage between these groups for other countries in the survey. Poor access to career guidance for the unemployed in Latin America likely reflects a lack of subsidised career guidance offered by the public employment service (see Chapter 4). To tackle these barriers to equal access, countries should consider expanding public career guidance provision to offer affordable or free high quality career guidance services to vulnerable adults (see Chapter 4) and designing financial measures to reduce the direct and indirect costs of career guidance for vulnerable adults (see Chapter 6).

The analysis also shows that many adults are not aware of career guidance services, which may in part be due to a lack of public information about them. Since they are not aware of career guidance services, adults rely more on informal channels, such as family and friends. Such reliance on family and friends for information risks compounding inequalities in the labour market. To improve access to formal career guidance opportunities, countries should:

- **Raise awareness about formal career guidance opportunities through media campaigns and active outreach to vulnerable groups.**

References

Chevalier, S. (2020), *Internet use in Latin America*, Statista, https://www.statista.com/topics/2432/internet-usage-in-latin-america/ (accessed on 16 February 2021). [4]

Gobierno de México (n.d.), *Observatorio Laboral*, http://www.observatoriolaboral.gob.mx/#/ (accessed on 4 March 2021). [2]

Nedelkoska, L. and G. Quintini (2018), "Automation, skills use and training", *OECD Social, Employment and Migration Working Papers*, No. 202, OECD Publishing, Paris, https://dx.doi.org/10.1787/2e2f4eea-en. [1]

OECD (2021), *Career Guidance for Adults in a Changing World of Work*, Getting Skills Right, OECD Publishing, Paris, https://dx.doi.org/10.1787/9a94bfad-en. [3]

Van Der Heyden, J. et al. (2017), *Additional weighting for education affects estimates from a National Health Interview Survey*, http://dx.doi.org/10.1093/eurpub/ckx005. [5]

Notes

[1] Online surveys have an inherent selectivity bias in that they over-represent the behaviour of individuals who tend to be online. These tend to be younger individuals with more formal education (Van Der Heyden et al., 2017[2]). Efforts were taken to mitigate this selectivity bias by imposing quotas on education, gender, region and age. See the survey methodology in the Annex for more details.

[2] Elementary occupations include cleaners and helpers; labourers in mining, construction, manufacturing and transport.

[3] In 2019, South America was the subregion in LAC with the largest internet penetration rate, with 72% of the population having access to this service (Chevalier, 2020[4]).

4 Provision and service delivery

Who do adults turn to for career guidance? The landscape of service providers in Latin America is diverse and includes private providers, education and training institutions, employers as well as public providers. This chapter maps the various providers, giving an overview of their characteristics and target groups. Drawing from survey evidence, it describes which channels are used to deliver career guidance (such as face-to-face, online, by telephone or instant messaging) and how adults learn about existing services. Finally, the chapter analyses how career guidance provision has changed in response to the COVID-19 pandemic.

In Brief

Guidance in Latin American countries is provided predominantly by private institutions in face-to-face sessions

How, where and by whom career guidance is provided determines its availability and accessibility. The variety of providers in Latin American countries has advantages but can also have disadvantages, depending on the setup. The main findings of this chapter include:

- The landscape of providers in each of the four Latin American countries (Argentina, Brazil, Chile and Mexico) covered by this report differs quite significantly from other countries that participated in the OECD 2020 Survey of Career Guidance for Adults (SCGA). Private career guidance providers are by far the most used among adults in Latin American countries (34%), followed by education and training providers (16%). Public employment services play a minor role in Latin American countries, accounting for only 9% of career guidance users compared with 27% across non-Latin American countries covered in the survey.

- The limited use of the PES in Latin America may be connected to limited public funding available for these services. At the same time, private career guidance services may be too costly for vulnerable groups to access unless they are subsidised.

- By far the most common way of interacting with a career guidance advisor in Latin American countries is face-to-face (50%). Guidance via telephone is used significantly less (16%), followed by online chat, videoconference and instant messaging.

- Striking mismatches appear between the actual and the preferred channels of guidance delivery. While only 5% of respondents currently use instant messaging for guidance, 26% would prefer to use this channel.

- The most common way for adults to learn about career guidance is via recommendations by friends or family members (a quarter of all respondents). The second most reported channel is one's employer, followed by the internet. The provision of information on guidance by the PES and other public career guidance services is more limited.

- The COVID-19 pandemic has resulted in an increase in demand for career guidance in Latin American countries: 51% of adults in Latin America reported having used guidance services more often than usual, either because they had more time or because they were navigating the ongoing changes, and 17% reported having used it less. While personal guidance via remote delivery is still being expanded in most of the Latin American countries in this survey, each country has developed online career guidance platforms offering automated support (e.g. tests, matching or application advice).

Introduction

Chapter 3 showed that there are large inequalities in access to career guidance across socio-economic groups in Latin American countries. In particular, unemployed adults are much less likely than employed adults to use career guidance services. Gaps in access to services could reflect insufficient provision and availability of publicly subsidised services, or poor awareness of available opportunities.

This chapter presents an overview of the different actors who offer career guidance services for adults in the four Latin American countries covered by the SCGA, and the delivery channels they use. It also discusses findings on the advertisement of career guidance and describes how the COVID-19 pandemic has influenced the use and provision of services.

Which actors deliver career guidance services to adults in Latin America?

In most Latin American countries, as elsewhere, career guidance is delivered by a range of different providers, including private providers, education and training institutions, dedicated public career guidance services, the public employment service (PES), as well as the social partners. Providers vary in their specific offers, whether they charge fees for their services or not, as well as which target groups they serve. While some providers focus on the unemployed, workers at risk, or highly educated professionals, others make their services open to anyone.

The following section maps different career guidance providers in Latin America, and the target groups they attend to. It also assesses general strengths and weaknesses associated with each type of provider.

Overview of different providers

Figure 4.1 gives an overview of the most important providers of career guidance services in the four Latin American countries covered by the survey. It shows that the largest group of adults who spoke with a career guidance advisor in the past 5 years, over one-third of adults (34%), did so through a private career guidance provider. Another 16% used career guidance services offered by an education or training provider, such as universities or institutions of continuous education and training; 13% of adults who used career guidance services did so through their employers. Dedicated public career guidance services accounted for 11% of users and around 9% of users spoke to a career guidance advisor of the public employment service. The remaining respondents consulted other providers, such as an employer group (6%), trade unions (5%) or associations (3%).

Figure 4.1. Providers of career guidance services for adults

Percentage of all adults who spoke to a career guidance advisor over the past 5 years, by provider

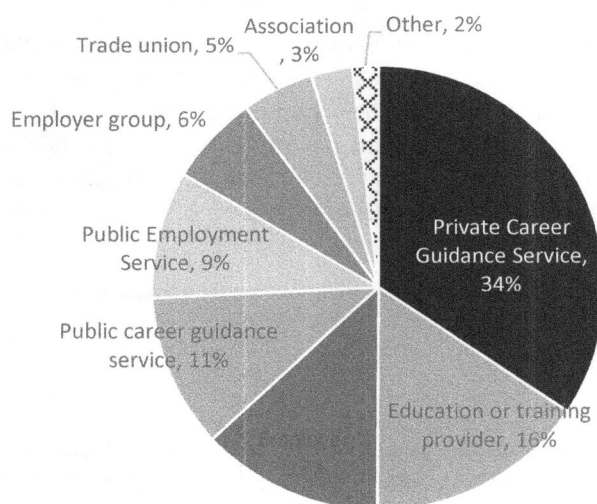

Note: Average of Argentina, Brazil, Chile and Mexico. Data refers to the last time the respondent spoke to a career guidance advisor.
Source: OECD 2020 Survey of Career Guidance for Adults (SCGA).

In comparison to other countries covered by the SCGA, a few observations stand out. Public employment services, for instance, play a relatively minor role in Latin America, serving only 9% of users. Across non-Latin American countries covered by the SCGA, the PES is the most frequent provider and accounts for 27% of career guidance services used by adults. Across the three European countries for which survey data is available (Germany, France and Italy) this percentage is even higher (36%).

Instead, in Latin America, private providers are paramount and account for more than one-third of career guidance services used by adults, much higher than in non-Latin American countries (21%), and European countries (19%) in the SCGA. A tentative explanation is that private career guidance providers in Latin America fill a gap left by less developed PES.

Adults gave different reasons for having chosen their respective career guidance provider (Figure 4.2). On average across the Latin American countries in the survey, 36% of respondents stated that their provider seemed to be the best quality, and 27% said that it was recommended to them by friends and family. Another 19% responded that they chose a particular career guidance provider because it was the only one they were aware of. Similar to the average of all countries covered by the SCGA (21%), this share is rather high and points to either limited availability of career guidance opportunities or poor awareness of existing ones.

Figure 4.2. Reasons for choosing a career guidance service

Percentage of adults who spoke with a career guidance advisor over the past 5 years, by reason of choosing a career guidance service over others

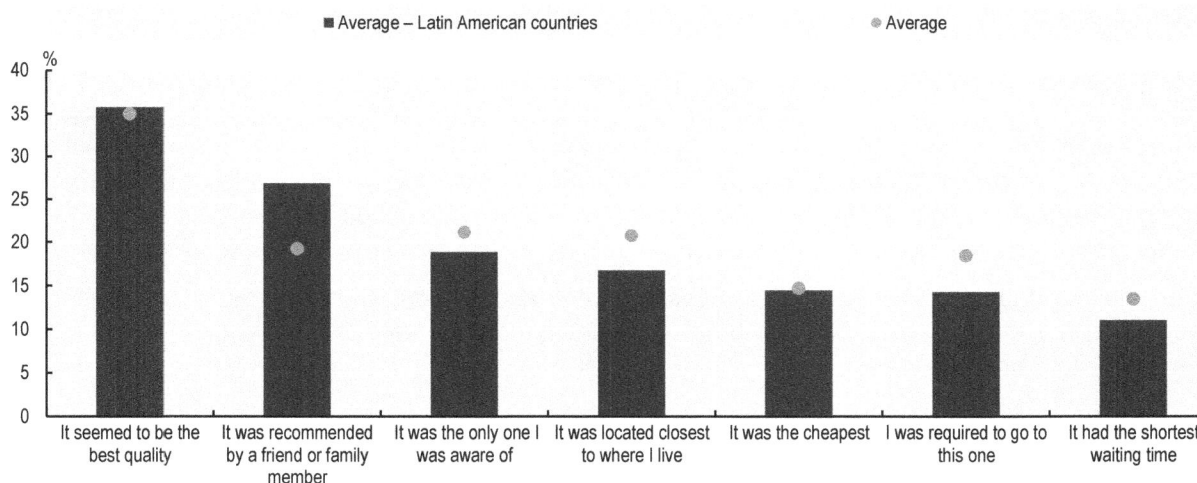

Note: Average – Latin American countries includes Argentina, Brazil, Chile and Mexico. Average includes Argentina, Brazil, Chile, France, Germany, Italy, Mexico, New Zealand and the United States. Respondents could choose more than one answer. Data refers to the last time the respondent spoke to a career guidance advisor.
Source: OECD 2020 Survey of Career Guidance for Adults (SCGA).

Private career guidance providers

One third of adults (34%) who used career guidance services in Latin America did so through a private career guidance provider (Figure 4.1). Private providers include a range of different institutions, such as specialised career consulting services or private labour intermediation agencies.

Across Latin American countries, the private career guidance sector is characterised by heterogeneous providers, with different target groups and professional practices. While detailed information on private career guidance services is scarce, there is potential for large differences between providers, both in terms of the type of services they provide and their quality (see Chapter 5). From a user perspective, and with no central overview platform available, this can make it difficult for adults to choose a private career guidance provider.

Adults may turn to a private career guidance provider if they are not eligible for free guidance provided by the PES (e.g. because they are in employment) or if they perceive PES guidance to be of low quality (see Chapter 5). Some people might also choose private services as an alternative because they do not have access to public career guidance offers in their local area. An important aspect to consider is that private services are commonly paid by the individual. Unless subsidised, career guidance from private providers may be costly and out of reach for certain groups, notably the unemployed or low-income workers.

There are different types of private career guidance providers that operate in Latin America. One group consists of for-profit individualised counselling services focused on coaching and career development of individuals. These providers typically target their services to higher-educated and higher-income adults who seek advice about career progression, changing jobs or training opportunities. This is considered closer in concept to the European/North American idea of career guidance services, which is otherwise rare in Latin American countries. As a result, in Latin American countries the holistic concept of career guidance is often associated with university-educated professionalsseeking guidance from private providers.

Another group of private providers focuses on labour intermediation services. These providers are either subcontractors of public employment services, or private agencies that offer outplacement services to companies that restructure or lay off some of their workforce. The provision of these services is regulated in most countries. In **Mexico**, for example, private labour market agencies are forbidden by law to charge a person for a successful job placement. Only additional services such as skills tests or training courses are fee-based. In **Argentina**, specialised agencies employ workers temporarily to place them with a third party *(empresas de servicios temporales)* and for jobseekers, these services have to be free by law. In **Chile**, these private providers are called *Agencias Privadas de Intermediación Laboral (APIL)*. Chile briefly experimented with a voucher programme that rewarded private agencies (APIL) for successful job matches, though the pilot was suspended in 2012 due to difficulties in measuring the programme's performance (ILO, 2015[1]). Generally across Latin America, private subcontractors tend to target lower-income groups and focus on providing basic skills training as well as information on employability.

Given the multitude of different private providers with various aims and services, a coherent career guidance policy is important. National career guidance strategies (see Chapter 6) can help to improve co-ordination among providers.

Education and training institutions

Education and training institutions provided guidance to 16% of SCGA respondents. In all four Latin American countries covered, universities are common providers of career guidance, although their services are mainly targeted at younger people who are enrolled in their programmes. Universities might also offer career guidance to adults, for whom these services sometimes include a fee. Adult learning institutions that offer continuous education and training often also provide career guidance to adults. National Training Institutes, for example, are established public agencies in charge of adult learning in Latin America, and are also involved in providing guidance around training for adults. While public investment in these institutes is sizable, problems of reach and effectiveness remain (OECD, 2020[2]).

Generally the availability and quality of career guidance services by education and training institutions varies between and within countries as well as across institutions. In **Argentina**, providers that belong to the Network of Continuing Education and Training Institutions (*Red de Formación Continua*) have to follow quality requirements introduced by the Ministry of Labour (see Chapter 5). The network consists of over 100 training centres across the country, which can be run by different providers including universities. The overall aim of having quality requirements in Argentina is to align training and skills development offered by different providers with local labour market needs as well as with a larger, strategic approach to skills and training.

Employers and employer groups

Generally, employers are in a good position to provide guidance to workers about their career development opportunities within the company, and employer groups tend to be well informed about sectorial skill needs. They can assist employees to reflect on their career goals and find suitable training options in order to develop their skills. In Latin America, 13% of adults who used career guidance services did so through their employers, and 6% through employer groups (Figure 4.1).

Few companies, however, have established mechanisms to provide career guidance to their employees. Where this is the case, companies usually focus on high-performing groups of employees, such as university graduates or managers. The majority of the workforce is not supported in the development of their career (CEDEFOP, 2008[3]). It can be presumed that the large number of informal workers in Latin American countries do not receive employer-provided career guidance services. Larger firms are generally more likely to support career guidance for their workers and to have a systematic approach to it compared with smaller firms. SMEs tend to have more limited resources, which often means that the provision of career guidance is more informal and depends on the individual manager.

Groups of employers in the same region or sector can co-ordinate career guidance activities for their employees. This is especially useful in cases where a region or sector is particularly affected by structural change. Often, employer groups provide both career guidance and education and training courses, such as the Training Centres of Economic Chambers or Business Associations (*Centros de Formación de Cámaras o Asociaciones Empresarias*) in **Argentina**, or the National Industrial Learning Service (*Serviço Nacional de Aprendizagem Industrial, SENAI*) in **Brazil**. SENAI is a network of non-profit professional schools established and maintained by the Brazilian Confederation of Industry, providing training and raising awareness about employment opportunities. Given that the implications of the COVID-19 pandemic differ across industries, a co-ordinated sector-based approach may be an effective way to keep workers close to the labour market, especially in the Latin American context where the social safety net is less generous.

Public employment services and dedicated public career guidance services

Compared with other countries in the SCGA, career guidance provided by the PES is less common in Latin America. Only 9% of career guidance users have received services from a PES provider across Argentina, Brazil, Mexico and Chile, while in non-Latin American countries covered by the SCGA, the PES is one of the main providers, serving 27% of career guidance users. This suggests that the role of the PES is more limited in Latin American countries. The overall importance of public career guidance services, including by the PES as well as dedicated public service providers, varies across Latin American countries. In Chile, public providers serve 26% of adult users of career guidance, while in Argentina they serve only 15%.

The eligibility for receiving PES career guidance services differs across countries, but in most Latin American countries unemployed adults, or specific vulnerable groups are the main target groups (Figure 4.3). Career guidance can even be mandatory for the unemployed in order to continue receiving unemployment benefits. Across all Latin American countries in the survey, the use of PES career guidance services was highest among the unemployed (16%). This share is much larger on average across all countries in the SCGA (35%). This means that although unemployed users of career guidance are the most important target group, they are much less covered by PES in Latin American countries compared with non-Latin American countries. Fourteen percent of individuals in informal employment who use career guidance services received them from PES providers, a share that is highest in Chile (23%). Only 10% of employed people and 8% of inactive individuals who are users of career guidance services receive them from PES providers.

Figure 4.3. Use of PES career guidance, by employment status

Percentage of adults who spoke with a PES career guidance advisor over the past 5 years, by employment status

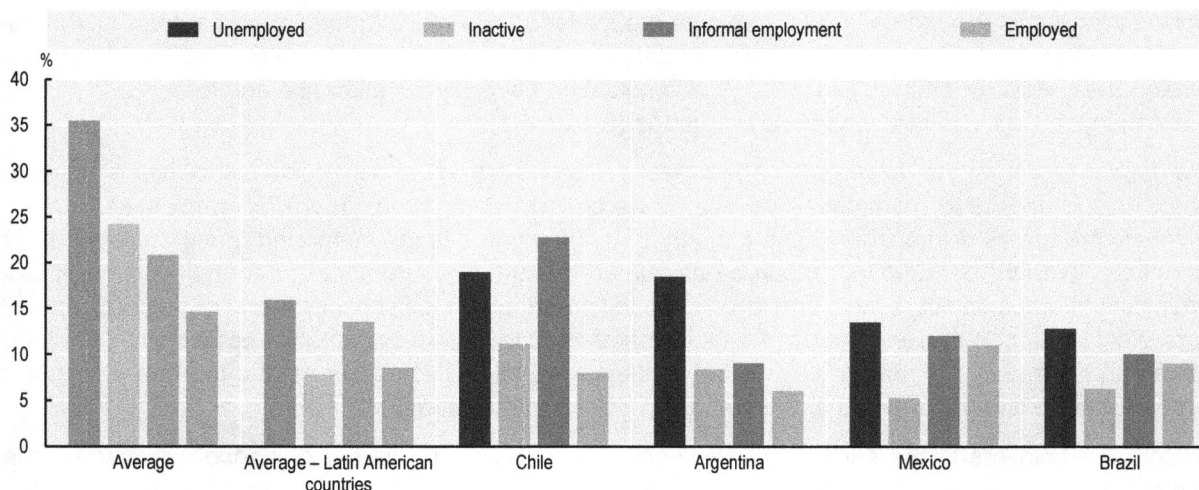

Note: Average – Latin American countries includes Argentina, Brazil, Chile and Mexico. Average includes Argentina, Brazil, Chile, France, Germany, Italy, Mexico, New Zealand and the United States. Data refers to the last time the respondent spoke to a career guidance advisor. The employed include permanent employees, temporary employees, employed without a contract, and self-employed. The inactive include retirees, those not working due to other reasons (e.g. looking after children, studying, illness or disability), and others. Employment status refers to when the person spoke to the career guidance advisor. The sample size of informal employment is smaller than 50 in Argentina and Brazil. The sample size of unemployment is smaller than 50 in Argentina and Brazil. The sample size of inactive is smaller than 50 in all four Latin American countries.
Source: OECD 2020 Survey of Career Guidance for Adults (SCGA).

The main responsibilities of the PES are typically job placement, active labour market policies and the management of unemployment insurance schemes. PES in all four Latin American countries provide labour intermediation services, called *Programa de Intermediación Laboral* in **Chile** or *Servicios de Vinculación Laboral* in **Mexico**. Helping unemployed people to find a job often involves assessing their skills, suggesting available training options, giving referrals to other services and providing labour market information and orientation. Some PES also have other, more particular, employment programmes that support the labour market integration of disadvantaged groups, for example low-skilled women or people with disabilities. Table 4.1 lists the PES in Argentina, Brazil, Chile and Mexico together with some indicators of their institutional capacity.

Latin American PES typically focus on the job placement aspect of labour intermediation, giving less attention to career guidance which ideally places a stronger emphasis on lifelong career development. The generosity and design of unemployment insurance plays an important role in this regard. In Mexico, where there is no unemployment insurance system, jobseekers are under pressure to quickly find a new source of income. Short-term goals of securing their livelihood, in such a situation, trump considerations of investing in skills training that would improve their labour market opportunities in the long run. Similarly, in Chile, the design of the unemployment insurance system – which ties funding of local employment offices to the three-month job placement rate – puts pressure on PES staff members to quickly place jobseekers in jobs.

Table 4.1. Public Employment Services in Latin America

Country	Original name of PES	English name of PES	Employment offices*	Staff members*	Reach	Budget
Argentina	*Red de Servicios Públicos de Empleo*	Public Employment Service Network	406 local offices and 168 branch units	1 785	502 156 people attended in 2019	-
Brazil	*Sistema Nacional de Emprego* (SINE)	National Employment System	27 regional offices, 1 600 local offices, and 400 branch units	1 460+ (number of local staff not available)	2.8 million people registered and 324 412 job placements in 2015	USD 20 949.7 milli on (in 2013)
Chile	*Servicio Nacional de Capacitación y Empleo, SENCE and Oficinas Municipales de Intermediación Laboral (OMIL)*	National Training and Employment Service and Municipal Labour Intermediation Offices	15 regional offices and 325 local offices.	712	358 527 people attended in 2019	USD 349.3 mi llion (in 2013)
Mexico	*Servicio Nacional de Empleo* (SNE)	National Employment Service	33 regional offices and 136 branch units (in 2021)	3 632	553 241 job placements and 5.1 million sessions in 2019 (*Servicios de Vinculación Laboral*)	USD 15.7 mill ion (in 2013)

Note: * Data is from 2015, unless specified otherwise. Reach refers to the number of people provided with labour intermediation services and may exclude more specialised employment programmes or digital services.
Source: OECD Secretariat, IDB, WAPES and OECD (2015[4]), *The World of Public Employment Services. Challenges, capacity and outlook for public employment services in the new world of work*, https://doi.org/10.1787/9789264251854-en; Ministry of Labour (2021[5]), *Programas de empleo y capacitación* (website), www.trabajo.gob.ar/estadisticas/Bel/programas.asp (accessed 13 January 2021); SENCE (2020[6]), *Intermediación Laboral año 2020*, www.sence.cl/601/articles-14036_archivo_04.pdf; ILO (2015[7]), *Public Employment Services in Latin America and the Caribbean: Chile*, www.ilo.org/wcmsp5/groups/public/---ed_emp/---emp_policy/---cepol/documents/publication/wcms_434598.pdf; Gobierno de México (2021[8]), *Servicio Nacional de Empleo* (website), www.empleo.gob.mx/sne (accessed 13 January 2021); Ministério da Economia (2016[9]), *Estatísticas SINE* (website), http://portalfat.mte.gov.br/programas-e-acoes-2/sistema-nacional-de-emprego-sine/rede-sine/estatisticas-sine/ (accessed 13 January 2021).

The quality of career guidance provision offered by the PES depends to some degree on its institutional capacity. According to the most recent international comparison, there are between 601-1000 unemployed for every PES staff member in Chile, Mexico and Argentina (OECD/IDB/WAPES, 2016[10]). This falls above the recommended caseload of 301-600 unemployed per staff member, and suggests that PES staff members likely face constraints in terms of time and budget. To optimally allocate limited resources, some OECD countries restrict access to intensive PES counselling services to the unemployed who are most in need of help (Desiere, Langenbucher and Struyven, 2019[11]; OECD, 2015[12]).

Trade unions

Trade unions are working in the interest of employees, and they may be in a good position to offer advice that is directly relevant for workers. They can potentially help individuals to progress and develop within their company, industry or sector. The involvement of trade unions in career guidance can include the direct provision of career guidance services to workers, as well as general training offers, awareness raising, advocacy or the referral to other providers.

In Latin America, 5% of adults have received career guidance from a trade union provider (Figure 4.1). The share of workers who are members of a union varies across countries. In 2014 it was highest in Argentina (28%), followed by Brazil (17%), Chile (17%) and Mexico (14%). Collective bargaining coverage rates follow a similar pattern, and are highest in Brazil (70%), followed by Argentina (51%), Chile (18%) and Mexico (10%) (ILOSTAT, 2021[13]). Surprisingly, high union membership or coverage does not translate to more frequent use of career guidance provided by trade unions. The country with the highest share of union-provided career guidance according to the SCGA is Mexico (8%), while it is lowest in Brazil (3%). This indicates differences in the range of services that unions provide across Latin American countries.

In some countries, unions have become important providers of career guidance. In **Argentina**, several unions run training centres (*Centros de Formación Profesional)* and are involved in the certification of skills in sectors such as construction, tourism and the automotive industry. Often, they provide guidance to workers about suitable learning opportunities (ILO, 2017[14]). Training centres are supported by contributions from the Ministry of Labour, Employment and Social Security. Other OECD examples include Unionlearn in the **United Kingdom**, a dedicated initiative on learning and skills by the British Trade Union Congress. Union Learning Representatives (ULRs) are contact points within companies, and their role is to promote the value of lifelong learning. They provide information, advice and guidance, carry out initial assessments of skills and link adults with training opportunities (OECD, 2021[15]).

Trade unions do not always provide career guidance themselves, but many are involved in governing bodies on employment and skills policy. Often these are tripartite institutions, with representatives of government, workers and employers. They decide on guidelines and resource allocation for labour intermediation programmes or training and skills strategies, while also monitoring their impact and proposing improvements in policy. One example is the CODEFAT (*Conselho Deliberativo do Fundo de Amparo ao Trabalhador*), which is a tripartite body attached to the Ministry of Economy in **Brazil** that co-ordinates labour intermediation services for adults. In **Chile**, labour unions are part of the governing body that heads *ChileValora*. *ChileValora* is a state body which evaluates, recognises, and certifies non-formal and informal skills, competencies, and knowledge of workers. It thereby links certification, training, and education in order to develop a system of lifelong learning for workers.

Trade unions can promote a range of other activities that support career guidance for adults, although their resources are often limited. In some OECD countries, trade unions run information and awareness-raising campaigns on career guidance or influence policy-making and advocate for better career guidance provision. Challenges for the involvement of trade unions in career guidance are a shortage of funding, other key priorities, and limited union coverage of workers, especially the most vulnerable ones.

Associations

Another group of providers in the Latin American context are non-profit associations, which serve 3% of career guidance users. These organisations tend to work for charitable causes, and offer support to improve the employability and labour market inclusion of particular groups of vulnerable populations. Some organisations also aim to strengthen research and practice of career guidance professionals in the given country. In **Brazil**, municipal governments run labour and employment programmes through non-governmental and social organisations (*organizações sociais, OS*). These are private non-profit associations that receive subsidies from the state to provide services of public interest. In Box 4.1, relevant examples of non-profit organisations across Latin America are highlighted.

Which channels are used for career guidance service delivery in Latin America?

Career guidance services can be delivered in different ways, including face-to-face (e.g. individual or group counselling), by telephone, through online chat, instant messaging, videoconference, or a mixed approach. Each approach has its strengths and weaknesses (see OECD (2021[18])).

In the Latin American countries covered by the SCGA, by far the most common way of interaction is face-to-face (50%), e.g. in the guidance provider's offices or at the adult's home. Face-to-face delivery is generally associated with better employment outcomes than remote alternatives (OECD, 2021[18]). The next most common channel is via telephone, which is used significantly less frequently (16%). Just as in the other countries covered by the SCGA, quite important mismatches appear between the actual and the preferred channel of guidance delivery (Figure 4.4). The most striking difference compared with the other countries covered in the survey is the high demand for guidance opportunities via instant messaging. This delivery channel is much more common in Latin America than in most OECD countries, in private as well as in business environments. It has some obvious advantages: Most applications are free of charge, it is easy to access and use, it uses very limited data volume, it can be used anywhere at any time and the exchanged information is recorded and saved automatically.

Figure 4.4. Actual and preferred channels of delivery of career guidance services

Percentage of adults who have spoken to a career guidance advisor over the past 5 years (actual), and percentage of respondents (preferred), by channel of delivery

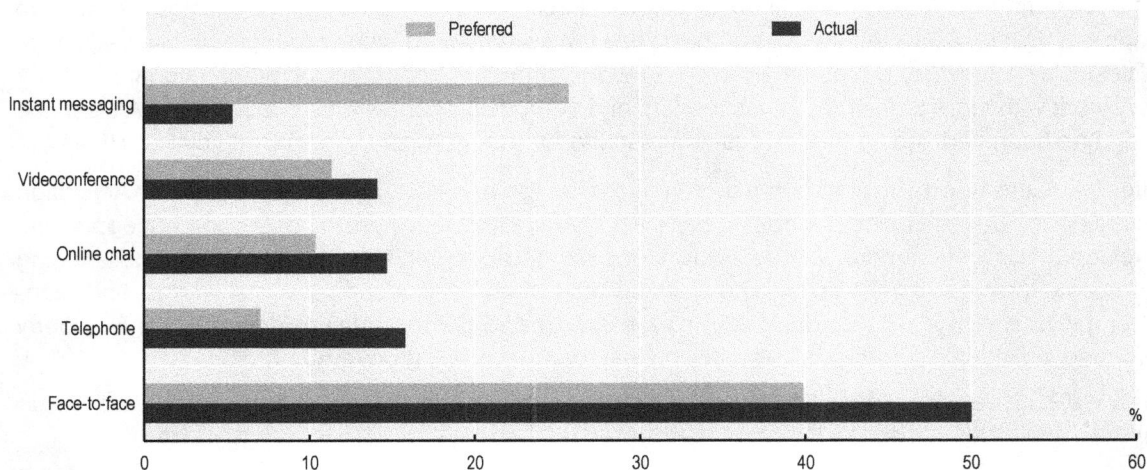

Note: Average of Argentina, Brazil, Chile and Mexico. Data refers to the last time the respondent spoke to a career guidance advisor. "actual" refers to the percentage of people who spoke to a career guidance advisor over the past 5 years. "preferred" refers to the percentage of all respondents, including both, users and non-users of career guidance services.
Source: OECD 2020 Survey of Career Guidance for Adults (SCGA).

How do adults learn about career guidance services?

The decision to take up guidance, as well as the choice of channel and provider of career guidance strongly depends on the adult's awareness of available options. As highlighted in Chapter 3, 33% of adults in the four Latin American countries reported not knowing that career guidance services existed. An additional 37% reported not feeling the need for guidance, possibly because they were not aware of its benefits. Raising awareness about career guidance opportunities and their potential benefits is thus a key challenge in these countries that should be tackled.

When asked 'Who informed you about the career guidance service you used?', the most common response by far was friends or family members (25%), followed by one's employer (19%) and the internet (11%) (Figure 4.5). The most striking difference in Latin America compared with other countries covered by the SCGA is the low reliance on the public employment service (5%), which is more than four times higher in non-Latin American countries (22%). This is in line with previous findings: the provision of career guidance by PES in Latin America is limited, and so is the information they provide about career guidance services. Given the low influence of the public services, it is probable that family and friends take over the role of advising adults about guidance services. These results suggest that public institutions in Latin American countries play a very small role in raising awareness about career guidance services for adults.

Figure 4.5. Advertisement of career guidance services for adults

Percentage of adults who spoke with a career guidance advisor over the past 5 years, by institution who notified them about the service

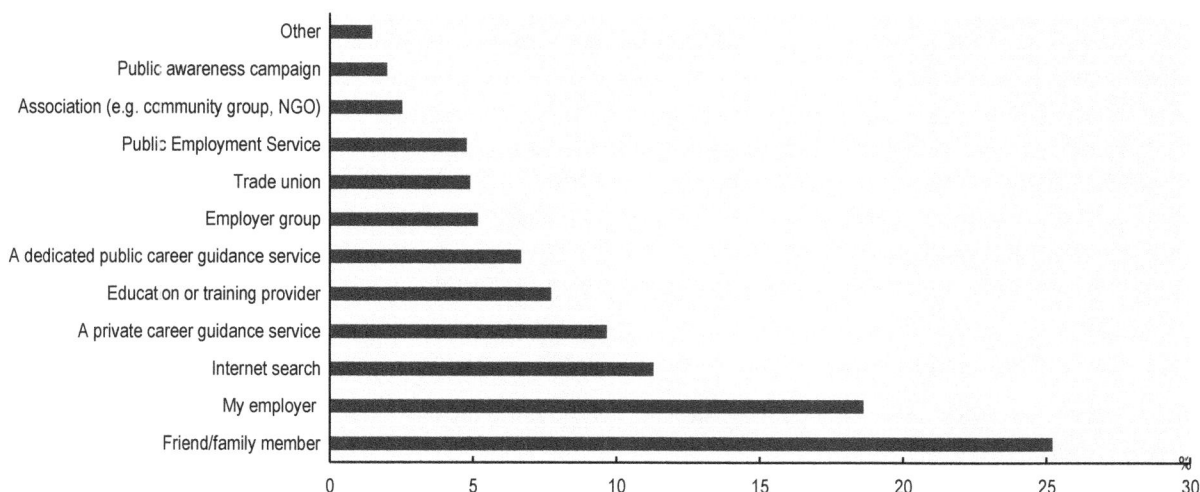

Note: Average of Argentina, Brazil, Chile and Mexico.
Source: OECD 2020 Survey of Career Guidance for Adults (SCGA).

All of the four Latin American countries in this review use a large variety of social media channels both to provide guidance directly and to advertise about available services. Use of social media in providing career guidance could be even further exploited by career guidance providers in Latin America, a region with the world's highest use of social media (Navarro, 2020[19]). The most popular social media channels in Latin America include Facebook, Twitter, Instagram, Youtube, LinkedIn, Flickr, and Soundcloud.[1] Through these channels adults can already access videos on interview preparation or presenting successfully placed candidates as an example to follow, podcasts informing about deadlines for application to training courses or tweets sharing links to different government programmes. These channels could be further exploited by providing personalised career guidance through instant messaging, which there seems to be demand for (Figure 4.4).

How have career guidance providers in Latin America adapted their offer in the context of the COVID-19 crisis?

Since early 2020, the COVID-19 pandemic has had a significant impact on people's working lives, employment status, and economic prospects. The Latin America and the Caribbean have been among the hardest-hit regions, experiencing a loss of working hours of 16% during 2020 (ILO, 2021[20]). In this context, career guidance can help unemployed adults find new employment and provides orientation for those that need to upskill. In response to this health crisis, most countries have introduced measures to adapt career guidance services to reduce in-person contact.

Demand for career guidance clearly increased in Latin American countries during the pandemic. The share of respondents who reported that their behaviour has not changed since the beginning of the pandemic is significantly lower than in other countries covered by the SCGA (43% vs. 66%).[2] 51% of adults in Latin America reported having used guidance services more often than usual and 17% reported having used it less (Figure 4.6). On net, this is likely to result in a dramatic increase in use of career guidance: from 33%

of adults using career guidance in a given year prior to the pandemic, up to an estimated 54% during and in the aftermath of COVID-19.

While demand for career guidance has increased during the pandemic in Latin American countries, remote delivery is catching up at a somewhat slower pace. As displayed in Chapter 3, 80-90% of adults in the Latin American countries use online information to find employment, education and training opportunities, which makes this channel particularly promising there. In **Chile**, for example, a cross-sector co-operation allowed for the continuation of the provision of career guidance services via online platforms. Chile is also reviewing all its available career guidance tools in order for them to be used online. However, adjusting the many tools currently used in face-to-face guidance to an online format may require more time and temporarily hamper access. In addition, several countries in this review reported that governments plan budget cuts in the area of career guidance for adults due to shifts in public funding following the COVID-19 pandemic. Fully or mainly replacing in-person guidance with cheaper digital offers may also seem tempting for the future, but bears the risk of losing adults who have no internet access or poor digital skills.

Figure 4.6. Change in the use of career guidance services during COVID-19

Percentage of adults responding whether behaviour regarding career guidance has changed in the context of the COVID-19 crisis

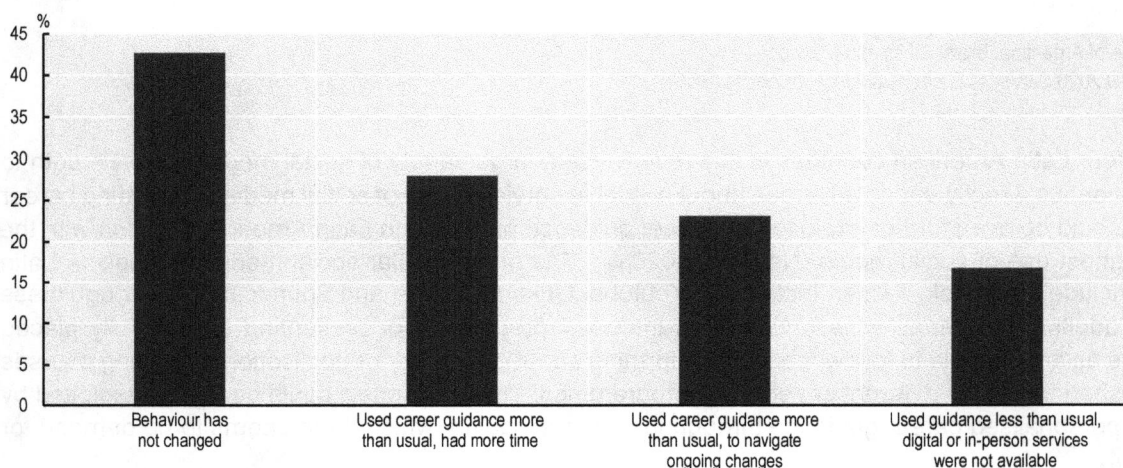

Note: Average of Argentina, Brazil, Chile and Mexico. Respondents could choose more than one answer.
Source: OECD 2020 Survey of Career Guidance for Adults (SCGA).

Recommendations

The results of the SCGA indicate that vulnerable groups such as the unemployed and low-educated are less likely to speak with a career guidance advisor than the reference population (see Chapter 3). These vulnerable groups face several barriers, while they could potentially benefit the most from career guidance services. Potential barriers include limited public service provision and the high cost of private provision. Public provision of career guidance encompasses both face-to-face and online delivery, both of which could be expanded:

- **Expand public provision (including PES) and associated funding to offer affordable or free high quality career guidance services to vulnerable adults.**

Face-to-face provision remains the most common channel of career guidance, and is generally associated with higher employment outcomes. But the COVID-19 pandemic calls for remote alternatives to face-to-face provision. Furthermore, the survey results suggest that individuals would like to access career guidance through alternative channels such as via instant messaging. Online career guidance platforms represent a cost-effective way to meet demand for professional career guidance. Existing platforms could be strengthened by providing personalised information based on skills assessments, by integrating information about job and training opportunities, and by giving users an opportunity to chat live with a counsellor directly on the platform:

- **Further expand the range of delivery channels available, and strengthen online career guidance platforms.**

References

ABOP (2021), *Associação Brasileira de Orientação Profissional. Quem somos*, https://abopbrasil.org.br/quem-somos/ (accessed on 15 January 2021). [23]

AMIA (2021), *Servicio de Empleo AMIA*, https://www.empleos.amia.org.ar/ (accessed on 15 January 2021). [16]

CEDEFOP (2008), *Career development at work. A review of career guidance to support people in employment.*. [3]

CODEFAT (n.d.), *CODEFAT – Portal do Fundo de Amparo ao Trabalhador*, https://portalfat.mte.gov.br/codefat/ (accessed on 27 November 2020). [22]

Desiere, S., K. Langenbucher and L. Struyven (2019), "Statistical profiling in public employment services. An international comparison", *OECD Social, Employment and Migration Working Papers*, OECD, http://dx.doi.org/10.1787/1815199X. [11]

Finn, D. (2011), *Sub-contracting in public employment services*, European Commission. [32]

Fundación Emplea (2021), *(No Title)*, https://www.fundacionemplea.cl/ (accessed on 15 January 2021). [17]

Fundación OCIDES (2021), *Fundación OCIDES. Desarrollo de carrera y orientación a lo largo de la vida*, https://www.ocides.org/ (accessed on 15 January 2021). [24]

Helbig, D., R. Mazzola and M. García (2015), *Servicios Públicos de Empleo en Argentina como pilar de apoyo a la política de empleo*, International Labour Organization, https://www.ilo.org/wcmsp5/groups/public/---americas/---ro-lima/---ilo-buenos_aires/documents/publication/wcms_452861.pdf (accessed on 13 January 2021). [21]

IDB, W. (2015), *The World of Public Employment Services. Challenges, capacity and outlook for public employment services in the new world of work.*, https://www.oecd-ilibrary.org/docserver/9789264251854-en.pdf?expires=1610719867&id=id&accname=guest&checksum=F7A5F8E54956347EA3B92220332E0212 (accessed on 15 January 2021). [25]

IDB, W. (2015), *The World of Public Employment Services. Challenges, capacity and outlook for public employment services in the new world of work.*, https://doi.org/10.1787/9789264251854-en (accessed on 15 January 2021). [4]

ILO (2021), *ILO Monitor. COVID-19 and the world of work. Seventh edition*, https://www.ilo.org/wcmsp5/groups/public/---dgreports/---dcomm/documents/briefingnote/wcms_767028.pdf (accessed on 25 January 2021). [20]

ILO (2017), *El futuro de la formación profesional en América Latina y el Caribe. Diagnóstico y lineamientos para su fortalecimiento.*, Oficina Regional de la OIT para América Latina y el Caribe. [14]

ILO (2015), *Public Employment Services in Latin America and the Caribbean. Chile.*, https://www.ilo.org/wcmsp5/groups/public/---ed_emp/---emp_policy/---cepol/documents/publication/wcms_434598.pdf (accessed on 13 January 2021). [7]

ILO (2015), *Public Employment Services in Latin America and the Carribean. Chile.*. [1]

ILOSTAT (2021), *Union membership*, Statistics on union membership, https://ilostat.ilo.org/topics/union-membership/ (accessed on 13 January 2021). [13]

México, G. (2021), *Servicio Nacional de Empleo*, Estadísticas Laborales, https://www.empleo.gob.mx/sne (accessed on 13 January 2021). [8]

Ministério da Economia (2016), *Estatísticas SINE – Portal do Fundo de Amparo ao Trabalhador*, http://portalfat.mte.gov.br/programas-e-acoes-2/sistema-nacional-de-emprego-sine/rede-sine/estatisticas-sine/ (accessed on 13 January 2021). [9]

Ministerio de Trabajo, E. (2013), *Actividades de capacitación en empresas privadas - Año 2013*, http://www.trabajo.gob.ar/downloads/estadisticas/eil/capem_Informe_Modulo_de_Capacitacion_EIL_2013.pdf (accessed on 15 January 2021). [27]

Ministry of Labour, E. (2021), *Programas de empleo y capacitación*, http://www.trabajo.gob.ar/estadisticas/Bel/programas.asp (accessed on 13 January 2021). [5]

Ministry of Labour, E. (2020), *Programas de empleo y capacitación*, http://www.trabajo.gob.ar/estadisticas/Bel/programas.asp (accessed on 13 January 2021). [31]

Navarro, J. (2020), *Social media usage in Latin America*, Statista, https://www.statista.com/topics/6394/social-media-usage-in-latin-america/ (accessed on 29 January 2021). [19]

OECD (2021), *Career Guidance for Adults in a Changing World of Work*, OECD Publishing, Paris, https://www.oecd-ilibrary.org/employment/career-guidance-for-adults-in-a-changing-world-of-work_9a94bfad-en (accessed on 8 January 2021). [18]

OECD (2021), *Career Guidance for Adults in a Changing World of Work*, Getting Skills Right, OECD Publishing, Paris, https://dx.doi.org/10.1787/9a94bfad-en. [15]

OECD (2020), *Effective Adult Learning Policies: Challenges and Solutions for Latin American Countries*, OECD Skills Studies, OECD Publishing, Paris, https://dx.doi.org/10.1787/f6b6a726-en. [2]

OECD (2019), *Getting Skills Right: Future-Ready Adult Learning Systems*, Getting Skills Right, OECD Publishing, Paris, https://dx.doi.org/10.1787/9789264311756-en. [28]

OECD (2019), *Getting Skills Right: Making adult learning work in social partnership*, http://www.oecd.org/employment/skills-and-work/adult- (accessed on 18 January 2021). [26]

OECD (2015), *Strengthening public employment services*. [12]

OECD/IDB/WAPES (2016), *The World of Public Employment Services: Challenges, capacity and outlook for public employment services in the new world of work*, Inter-American Development Bank, Washington, D.C., https://dx.doi.org/10.1787/9789264251854-en. [10]

SENCE (2020), *Intermediación Laboral año 2020*, http://www.sence.cl/601/articles-14036_archivo_04.pdf (accessed on 13 January 2021). [6]

Servicio Nacional de Empleo (2021), *Cobertura del SNE | Portal del Empleo*, https://www.empleo.gob.mx/sne/cobertura (accessed on 13 January 2021). [30]

Servicio Nacional de Empleo (2020), *Programa de Apoyo al Empleo (PAE) | Portal del Empleo*, Estadísticas Laborales, https://www.empleo.gob.mx/sne/acciones-vinculacion-laboral (accessed on 13 January 2021). [29]

Notes

1 www.gov.br/pt-br/canais-do-executivo-federal, https://sence.gob.cl/personas/orientacion-laboral, www.observatoriolaboral.gob.mx, www.portalempleo.gba.gov.ar

2 Data collection in Chile, France, Germany, Italy, New Zealand and the United States took place from mid-June to early July 2020, while in Argentina, Brazil and Mexico it took place in November 2020.

5 Quality and impact

What distinguishes high-quality career guidance services and how can the current provision of these services in Latin American countries be improved? This chapter analyses survey evidence of adults' satisfaction with available services as well as the perceived training and employment outcomes of career guidance. It then reviews approaches to raise the quality of services, including using high-quality labour market information, tailoring services to adults' needs, standardising staff training and qualifications, certifying career guidance providers and monitoring outcomes.

In Brief

Promoting quality career guidance for adults in Latin America

A recent OECD report on adult career guidance systems laid out three components of quality career guidance: high-quality labour market information; tailored to an individual's needs; and provided by professional career guidance advisors. It also suggested several ways of to promote quality assurance in career guidance by: standardising training and qualifications of career guidance advisors; certifying providers against quality standards; and monitoring outcomes. The main findings from this chapter are:

- Overall satisfaction with career guidance services in Latin American countries is high (88%). Furthermore, most users (82%) say that they experienced a positive outcome (e.g. enrolling in a training programme, finding a new job, getting a promotion) in the six months following career guidance. However, only a third of these adults attribute the positive outcomes to the career guidance they received. Adults are much more likely to report positive outcomes if they receive a personalised career development roadmap as an output of career guidance. They are also more likely to report employment outcomes if they receive services face-to-face, and if services are provided through their employer or an employer group. Enrolment in education and training participation is more likely if career services are provided by an education and training institution.

- Career guidance advisors in the countries under review rely heavily on online platforms to keep them up-to-date about labour market developments. Mexico is the only country where career guidance advisors in the public employment service receive briefings about labour market developments.

- In Latin American countries, as in most OECD countries, the job of 'career guidance advisor' is not a regulated profession. Countries in this review have taken steps towards streamlining the qualifications and competencies of career guidance advisors, though these steps have fallen short of developing competence frameworks.

- Some 62% of adult users reported receiving a personalised career development roadmap as an output of guidance, despite roadmaps not being a required output of public programmes. This is a higher share than the average across all countries in the survey.

- Interviews are the most common method for assessing an adult's skills in Latin America, as in other countries. Self-reported information is often used in tandem with interviews and tends to focus on qualifications and occupational history. Skills profiling tools, including direct assessment tests, which more objectively assess an individual's skills against a benchmark, are not used by career guidance advisors in Latin America. Given that they cover both skills acquired formally or informally, such tools may be particularly useful to provide guidance to adults in informal employment and those without formal qualifications.

- Quality standards in career guidance are rare in Latin America, with Argentina being the only country that applies a comprehensive quality management system to career guidance provision.

- Monitoring of career guidance provided by the public employment service is carried out by government bodies in Chile, Argentina and Mexico. Mexico also monitors the outcomes of educational guidance as part of its monitoring of education services more generally.

Introduction

As outlined in Chapter 2, the labour market in Latin American countries is characterised by high inequality, a high share of informal employment, and high rates of over-qualification. By helping individuals make more informed employment and training decisions, career guidance can mitigate skills imbalances and potentially help individuals to move into more secure employment. It can help to reduce inequality by making sure all individuals have access to quality labour market and training information and guidance, regardless of their socio-economic situation. These positive outcomes are only possible, however, if services are of high quality.

This chapter reviews survey evidence on the impact of career guidance in Latin America, focusing on reported satisfaction and perceived employment and training outcomes. It compares Argentina, Brazil, Chile and Mexico along three different dimensions of quality career guidance: the use of high-quality labour market information; the implementation of a tailored approach to guidance provision; and the professional requirements for career guidance advisors. It also discusses two types of quality assurance mechanisms: the certification of providers against quality standards; and the monitoring of outcomes.

How satisfied are adults with career guidance services in Latin American countries?

According to the SCGA, most adults in Latin America report being satisfied with the career guidance they receive. Some 87% of adults in Latin American countries are satisfied with the career guidance they received, which is on par with the average across all countries in the SCGA (Figure 5.1). A similar share of adults say that guidance is well-informed (88%), while a lower share report that it is well-targeted to their individual needs (81%). Perceived satisfaction is highest in Brazil (91%) and Mexico (89%), and just below average in Argentina (86%) and Chile (82%).

While user satisfaction is a helpful indicator of quality, cross-country comparisons should be interpreted with caution. User satisfaction surveys are highly subjective, and there is room for cultural bias. A review of global user satisfaction surveys found that respondents from Latin America are more likely than those elsewhere to choose ratings at the extreme ends of a scale (for a 1-10 scale, this generally means 1-4 or 9-10) (Wilcock, 2021[1]). Given these limitations, user satisfaction rates are likely most informative when looked at as a trend within a particular country.

Figure 5.1. User satisfaction with career guidance

Percentage of adults who received career guidance services in the last five years

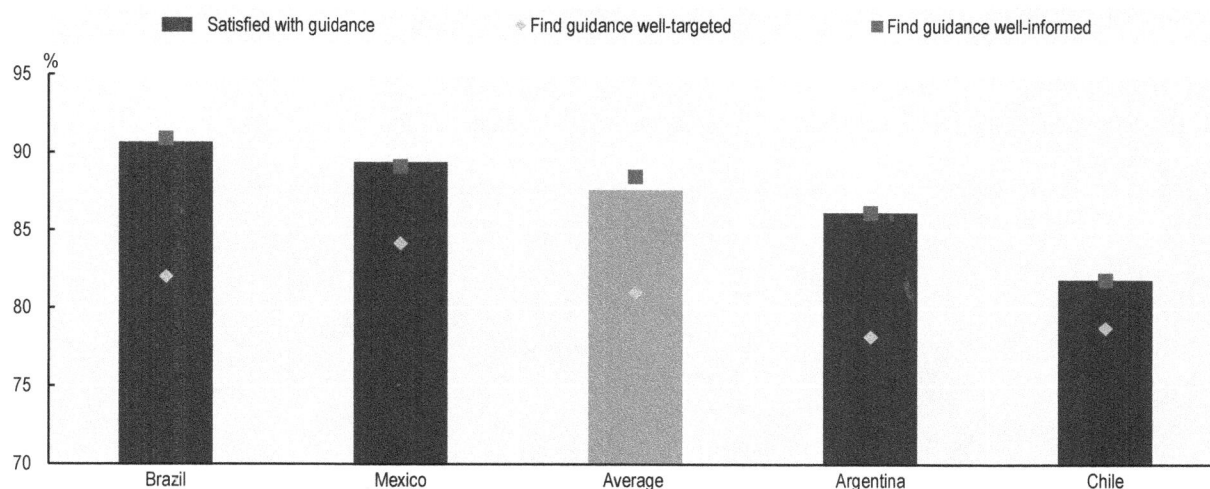

Note: Average refers to all nine countries covered by the SCGA.
Source: Survey of Career Guidance for Adults (SCGA).

What are the outcomes of guidance in Latin American countries?

Users of career guidance in Latin America are more likely to report that they experienced an improvement in employment or training outcomes within six months of receiving the service, compared to adults in other countries. The large majority of adults in Latin American countries (82%) confirmed that they had experienced an employment or training outcome – higher than the average for all countries in the SCGA (70%). The most common outcomes were progressing in one's current job (37%), enrolling in training or education (26%), or finding a new job (26%). About 12% of adults reported that they had moved from informal to formal employment.

However, while most adults reported an employment or training outcome, a smaller share attributed the change to having received career guidance (Figure 5.2). Only about a third (32%) of adults in Latin America said that career guidance was useful in achieving employment and training outcomes. While this is a higher share compared to the average of all countries in the survey (27%), it suggests there is room for improving the quality of career guidance services.

Table 5.1 summarises results from a regression of the likelihood of achieving employment or training outcomes after receiving career guidance, while controlling for a set of individual, job and firm characteristics. The regression pools data from the four Latin American countries (Argentina, Brazil, Chile, and Mexico). However, coefficients are not significantly different from those obtained when including all countries in the regression, implying that the following results are not unique to Latin America:

- Two factors stand out as being highly associated with achieving positive employment outcomes: receiving a personalised career development roadmap (increases the likelihood by 26%), and using services delivered by an employer or employer group (both increase the likelihood by 12%, relative to services delivered by the PES). Having face-to-face interaction with a career guidance advisor is also associated with a higher likelihood of achieving positive employment outcomes (5% higher than remote alternatives).

- An adult is more likely to enrol in an education or training programme after receiving career guidance from an education or training provider (18% higher than when provided by the PES), followed by an employer group (10% higher). Receiving a personalised career development roadmap also raises the likelihood of enrolling in an education or training programme by 10%

Figure 5.2. Employment and training outcomes of career guidance

Percentage of adults who received career guidance in the last five years, by reported outcome

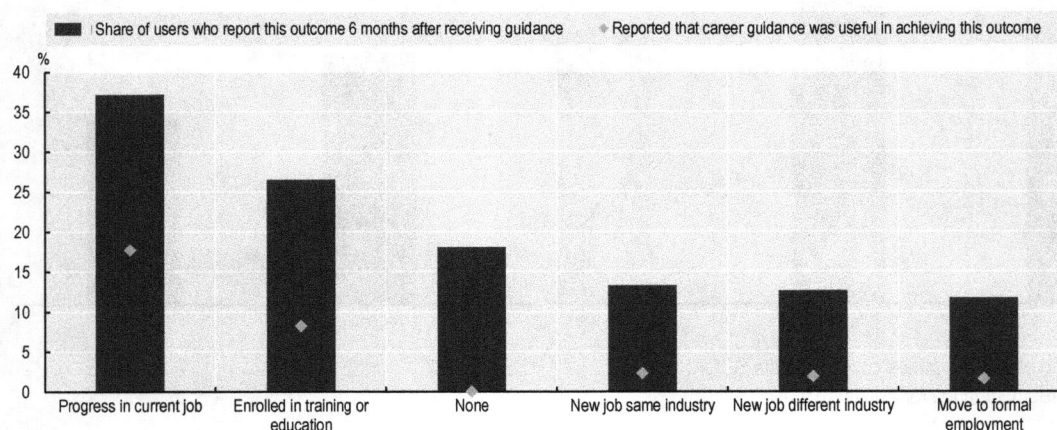

Note: Average of Argentina, Brazil, Chile and Mexico. Respondents could choose more than one answer. Data refer to the last time the respondent spoke with a career guidance advisor.
Source: Survey of Career Guidance for Adults (SCGA).

Table 5.1. Employment, education and training outcomes of career guidance in Latin America

Marginal effects from a probit regression

	Labour market outcome		Education outcome	
	Respondents who used career guidance in the last 5 years		Respondents who used career guidance in the last 5 years	
Face-to-face (ref=remote delivery)	0.051	*	0.031	
Provider type (ref=Public employment service)				
Private career guidance provider	-0.020		0.054	
Dedicated public career guidance service	-0.004		0.073	
My employer	0.124	***	0.010	
Trade union	0.049		0.031	
Employer group	0.124	**	0.097	**
Education or training provider	-0.049	**	0.184	***
Association	-0.058		0.029	
Other	-0.148	*	0.049	
Personalised career development roadmap	0.255	***	0.099	***
Observations	1712		1712	
Pseudo R^2	0.207		0.049	

Note: The regression pools responses from adults in Argentina, Brazil, Chile and Mexico. The dependent variable "Employment outcome" takes value 1 if a respondent reported at least one of the following outcomes: "Found a new job in the same industry", "Found a new job in a different industry", "Progressed in my current job (e.g. got a promotion)", or "Moved from informal employment (without a contract) to formal employment," and 0 otherwise. The dependent variable "Education outcome" takes value 1 if the respondent reported that they "Enrolled in a new education or training programme "and 0 otherwise. The regression includes additional controls for country, age, place of residence, education, gender, employment status, migration, firm size and contract type. The table reports marginal effects, i.e. percentage change in the outcome variable following a change in the relevant explanatory variable. Marginal effects for categorical variables refer to a discrete change from the base level. *,**,***: statistically significant at the 1%, 0.1%, and 0.01% level, respectively.
Source: OECD 2020 Survey of Career Guidance for Adults (SCGA).

Policies to promote high-quality career guidance services in Latin America

A recent OECD report laid out three components of quality career guidance: it relies on high-quality labour market information, is tailored to an individual's needs, and is provided by professional career guidance advisors (OECD, 2020[2]). The report also suggested several ways of promoting quality assurance in career guidance: by standardising training and qualifications of career guidance advisors, certifying providers against quality standards and monitoring outcomes.

This section compares Argentina, Brazil, Chile and Mexico along these quality dimensions. It draws good practice examples from OECD countries when applicable.

Using high-quality labour market information

According to the SCGA, adults in Latin America were more likely to receive some types of labour market information than others during their interaction with a career guidance advisor (Figure 5.3). Just over half received information about education and training programmes (53%), compared with 48% in all countries covered by the SCGA. This was followed by information about sectors in high or low demand (35% vs. 32% in all countries), job vacancies (30% vs. 35%) and sectors forecasted to be in high or low demand in the future (26%, similar to the overall average). Fewer adults reported receiving information on the quality of training providers (21%) or financial support available for training (12%).

Career guidance advisors need to keep up-to-date about labour market developments to provide quality career guidance. In **Chile**, for instance, career guidance advisors who are part of the *Programa de Intermediación Laboral* are expected to consult an online platform which is regularly updated with job vacancies by companies, and with training opportunities by SENCE. Similar websites exist in Brazil and Mexico, providing up to date labour market information. In some cases, training is provided to career guidance advisors. As part of **Mexico**'s Employment Support Programme, advisors receive training on the behaviour of local and regional labour markets.

Figure 5.3. Type of information that adults receive from career guidance advisors

Percentage of adults who spoke to a career guidance advisor over the past five years, by type of information received

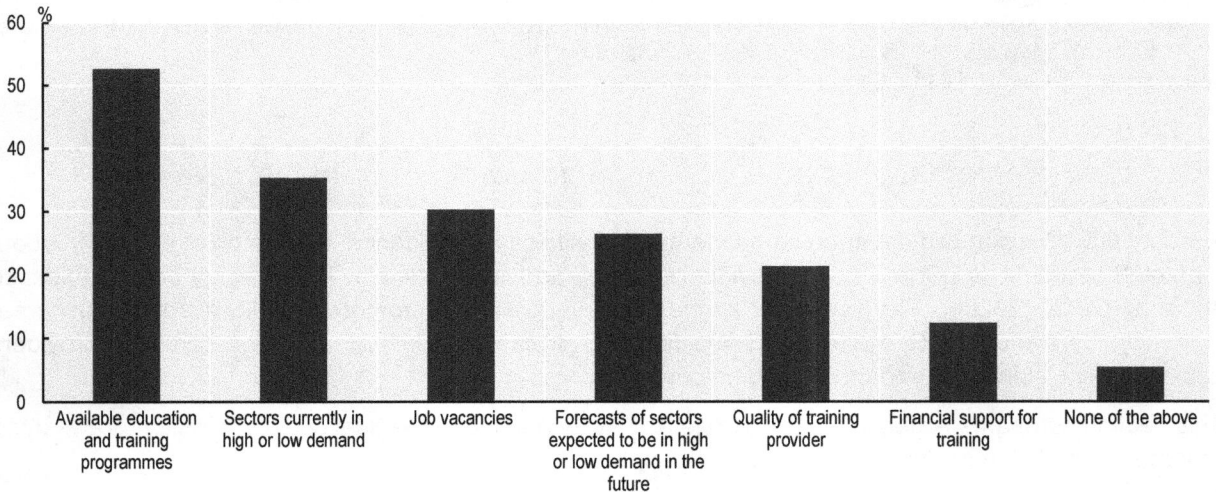

Note: Average of Argentina, Brazil, Chile and Mexico. Respondents could choose more than one answer. Data refer to the last time the respondent spoke to a career guidance advisor.
Source: Survey of Career Guidance for Adults (SCGA).

Tailoring career guidance services to adults' needs

While a high share of adults in Latin American countries report that career guidance is tailored to their needs (81%), a lower share report receiving a personalised career development roadmap (62%). A personalised career development roadmap – otherwise known as an individual training plan or personal action plan – spells out the activities needed to reach one's career and training objectives. Receiving such an individualised roadmap increases the likelihood of achieving positive employment outcomes after career guidance by 25%, and of enrolling in an education or training programme by 7% (OECD, 2021[3]). It does so by empowering adults to take informed action towards their goals.

Adults in Brazil and Mexico were more likely than those in Argentina and Chile to receive a personalised career development roadmap (Figure 5.4). But roadmaps are not a required output of any of the publicly subsidised career guidance programmes in the countries in this review, while this is the case in some OECD countries. For example, in **Australia**, adults who participate in the Career Transition Assistance programme must receive a personalised "Career Pathway Plan" that provides tailored information on retraining opportunities in line with labour market needs.

Figure 5.4. Personalised career development roadmap

Percentage of adult career guidance users who report receiving a career development roadmap

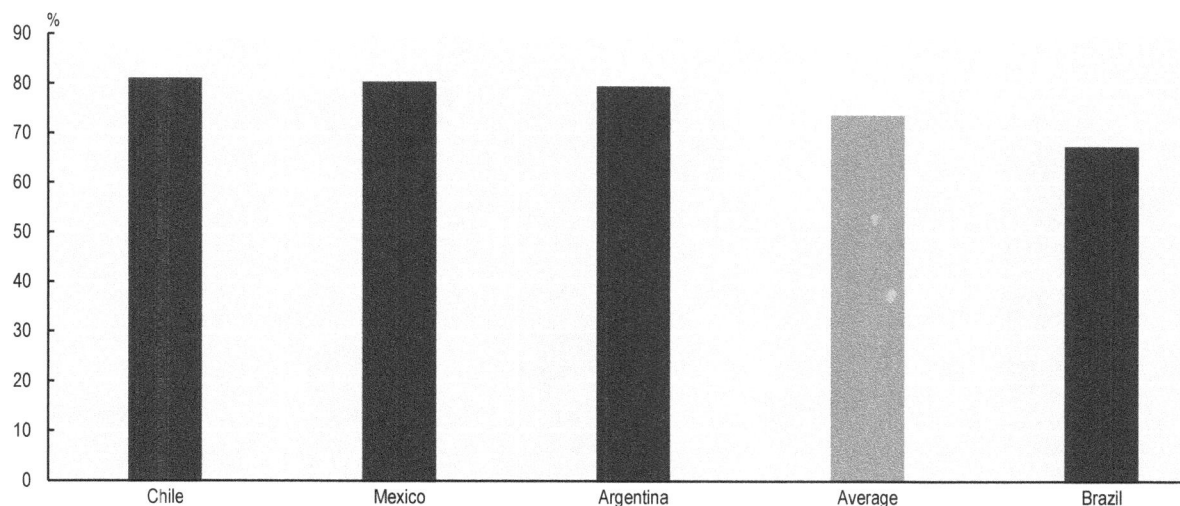

Note: Average refers to all nine countries covered by the SCGA.
Source: Survey of Career Guidance for Adults (SCGA).

A necessary starting point in providing personalised career and training pathway advice for adults is to conduct a thorough assessment of their skills. As in other countries, interviews are the most common method for assessing an adult's skills in Latin American countries (Figure 5.5). Some 68% of adults were asked about their skills and experience, and another 21% were asked about their certificates or qualifications. Though common, interviews are subjective methods for assessing someone's skills and they tend to rely heavily on job history and educational qualifications as a proxy for skills. They are also potentially costly in terms of staff time required to conduct them.

Using tests to assess an individual's skills can provide an alternative or complement to interviews, though such tests are not widely used in public programmes in Latin American countries. Some 46% of adults who spoke with a career guidance advisor in Latin American countries were asked to complete a test to assess their skills. In **Chile**, career guidance advisors in the *Programa de Intermediación Laboral* complement interviews with various self-assessment tests. For the most part, these self-assessment tests try to capture the individual's personality type and help them to narrow down their interests and preferences.[1] In **Mexico**, adults can complete skills and vocational tests on the public employment support website, *Observatorio Laboral*.

Skills profiling tools go a step beyond self-assessments. They involve completing a test that can be graded against an answer key, making it more objective. These tools provide a measure of what an individual can actually do, and do not discriminate between skills acquired formally or informally. This makes them particularly effective in supporting adults in informal employment or those without formal qualifications. A handful of public employment services have started using skills profiling tools to support flexible pathways and to redeploy adults from declining to growing jobs and sectors. The PES in **Italy** and **Spain** piloted an online version of the OECD's Survey of Adult Skills to test the literacy, numeracy and digital skills of jobseekers (Education and Skills Online).

Figure 5.5. Methods for assessing skills

Percentage of adults who spoke with a career guidance advisor in the past five years, by method used to assess their skills

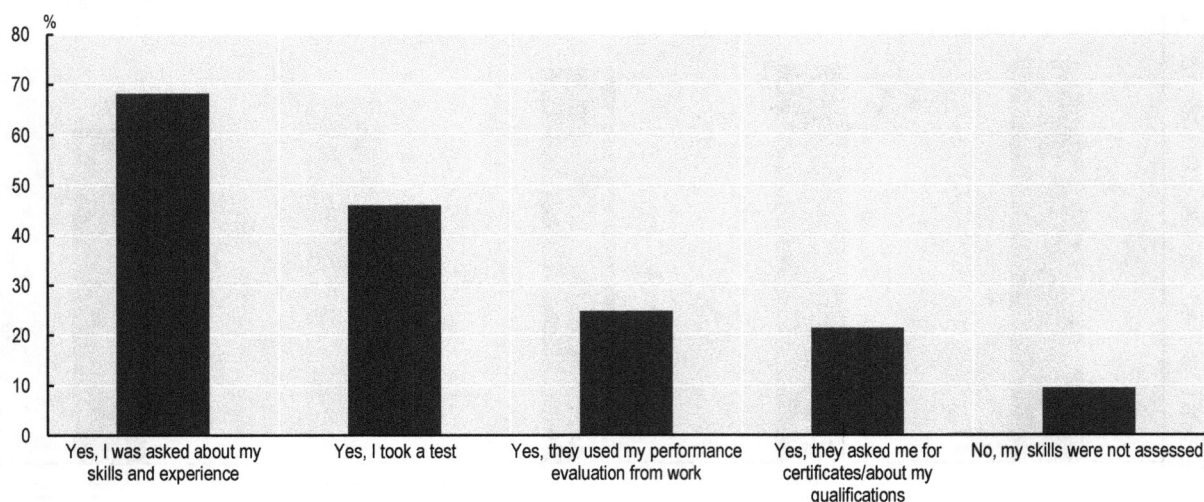

Note: Average of Argentina, Brazil, Chile and Mexico.
Source: Survey of Career Guidance Advisors (SCGA).

Standardising training and qualifications of career guidance advisors

The training, qualifications and competencies of career guidance advisors are key for high-quality service delivery. Defining standardised requirements for this occupation can help to improve career guidance services, and make their quality more coherent across different providers. In Latin American countries, as in most OECD countries, the job of 'career guidance advisors' is not a regulated profession. No specialised training course, certificate or license exists for this occupational group. Nevertheless, working as a career guidance advisor in Latin American countries generally requires a certain level of training and qualification, usually a tertiary degree.

As in other countries, the qualifications and competencies of career guidance staff in Latin America differ according to the type of provider. Compared to career guidance professionals working for private providers, counsellors working for public employment services tend to have lower and less specialised qualification requirements, as their services are often broader and not restricted to career guidance. Furthermore, the variance in local governance and institutional capacity of public employment services that is common in Latin American countries is likely to also cause differences in staff qualifications. Career guidance advisors working for private providers or at universities, on the other hand, usually have higher or more specialised qualification requirements, such as tertiary-level degrees in psychology.

If career guidance advisors do not receive specialised training but instead hold general tertiary degrees, the risk is that they might lack crucial skills and knowledge to provide high-quality career guidance. This can also result in a varying standard of practice across providers. To address this, OECD (2004) recommended establishing competency frameworks as a first step to improve and standardise career guidance services, which many countries have since developed (OECD, 2021[3]). Competency frameworks define what career guidance advisors should know and do, and they form a foundation for designing training and qualifications. Examples from other countries show that introducing competency frameworks for career guidance advisors can be an important step towards more coherent and high-quality service provision. Examples from Austria and Canada are provided in Box 5.1.

Latin American countries have taken steps towards streamlining the qualifications and competencies of career guidance advisors, though these steps have fallen short of developing competence frameworks. In **Argentina**, general efforts to reduce disparities and streamline service provision across public employment offices included the improvement of training provided for counsellors. **Mexico** has a general competence framework for all providers of public services (*atención al público*). While this framework applies to career guidance advisors working for the public employment service (*SNE – Servicio Nacional de Empleo*), it is not a dedicated competence framework for this professional group. In **Brazil**, there is so far no regulation of the practice of career guidance. Professionals from various fields of knowledge work as career advisors, but most are psychologists. Several initiatives have aimed to regulate and professionalise career guidance occupations, such as a competence framework proposal developed based on the IAEVG (International Association for Educational and Vocational Guidance) model. None of these approaches, however, has been widely implemented.

Continuing professional development helps advisors develop and maintain their skills and knowledge in the face of changes in the labour market and in technology. Refresher training for career guidance advisors can help to uphold the quality of career guidance in the face of constant technological change. The need for career guidance advisors to develop or strengthen digital skills became especially apparent in the COVID-19 pandemic, as career guidance service delivery came to a halt or shifted online.

Box 5.1. Competency frameworks for career guidance advisors in Austria and Canada

The public employment service in **Austria** uses the European Career Guidance Certificate (ECGC), which is based on the MEVOC standards (Quality Manual for Educational and Vocational Counselling). These standards were developed as a project of the European Union under the leadership of Austria (ibw – *Institut für Bildungsforschung der Wirtschaft*) in co-operation with 19 partner institutions from nine countries. They describe quality standards for educational and vocational counsellors. Based on the MEVOC standards, a competence grid was developed with 35 required competences in the following four areas: education, career, counselling practice, personality and ICT competences. To achieve the ECGC, counsellors can complete an online test and an assessment centre.

The **Canadian** Standards and Guidelines for Career Development Practitioners (S&G) determine the competences needed to provide high-quality career guidance. It was the first competence framework developed internationally and served as a model for other countries. The S&Gs provide a foundation for designing training, to provide quality assurance to the public, to recognise and validate the skill sets of practitioners in the field, and to create a common voice and vocabulary for career development. Competencies are organised in three areas: core competencies, specialisation competencies and ethical principles. Five provinces in Canada have developed professional certifications linked to the S&Gs (British Colombia, Alberta, Ontario, New Brunswick and Nova Scotia). The competence framework is currently being updated and expanded based on national consultations. A new national professional credential, tied to the new competence framework, is also being developed.

Source: OECD 2020 Policy Questionnaire 'Career Guidance for Adults'.

Certifying providers against quality standards in service delivery

Quality standards help to promote high-quality service delivery across the country. They can govern several or all aspects of service delivery including professional standards, partnerships, labour market information, client satisfaction, evaluation and leadership (Dodd et al., 2019[4]).

Quality standards for career guidance in Latin American countries tend to focus on public provision of services. In **Argentina**, for example, a quality management system (QMS) with a customer-based approach for public employment services has been developed by the Argentinian Standards Institute (IRAM) in accordance with ISO 9 000 standards. The Argentinian Ministry of Employment and Social Security (MTEySS) also defined quality criteria, which included: a clear office structure, a marketing strategy, profiling methods, capacity for providing job and vocational counselling. If these criteria are met, a quality management certificate is issued. In 2015, 72 employment offices had been awarded the certificate (ILO, 2015[5]). On a less comprehensive scale, public funding of municipal employment offices (OMIL) in **Chile** is tied to achieving employment outcomes, as measured by a three-month job placement indicator.

In **Argentina,** providers that belong to the Network of Continuing Education and Training Institutions (*Red de Formación Continua*) also have to follow quality requirements introduced by the Ministry of Labour. These institutions can be run by unions, business associations, universities or non-for-profit providers. Many of them have been strengthened as part of a quality certification process, with the aim of aligning training and skills programmes with local labour market demand.

Monitoring outcomes

Monitoring outcomes of career guidance helps providers to evaluate and improve their performance, and holds the system to account. Common types of outcomes measured include user satisfaction, employment, wages, unemployment benefit receipt, and training participation.

In Latin American countries, career guidance programmes offered by the public employment service are monitored and evaluated by government bodies. In **Argentina**, the quality of public employment programmes is monitored by the Ministry of Labour, Employment and Social Security through its labour market observatories and in support of the quality management system (QMS) discussed above. Argentina's Office of Studies and Statistics prepares and publishes reports about the effectiveness of employment programmes. Similarly, in **Mexico**, the National Council for the Evaluation of Social Development Policy (CONEVAL) monitors the outcomes of SNE's programmes, and publishes data on its website. Indicators focus on the number of jobseekers who receive support. In **Chile**, the SENCE head office monitors the Regional Directorates, which in turn monitor the OMIL offices. SENCE tracks three main indicators: the number of users of labour intermediation services, labour market placements, and user satisfaction.

In **Mexico**, monitoring of career guidance outcomes is also carried out as part of the evaluation of education services more generally. A national evaluation of the results of each educational programme and project is carried out in the State Institutes and Delegations (*Institutos y Delegaciones Estatales*). Results of the evaluations are considered in the process of analysis and approval of the federation's expenditure budget for the following fiscal year. These evaluations are conducted by academic and research institutions or organisations that specialise in adult education, and that meet minimum requirements set by the ministry.

Brazil stands out among the countries in this review for its lack of systematic monitoring practices for career guidance programmes. Brazil has data in place that could be better exploited to monitor the impacts of guidance. Rich administrative data from the Annual Social Information Report (RAIS) could track inputs and outputs of various policies, including guidance and labour intermediation programmes, especially when combined with other databases such as the General Register of Employed and Unemployed Individuals (CAGED). As argued in other analyses, these data could be used to develop a comprehensive monitoring and evaluation system focused on tracking outcomes such as employability (Joana Silva, 2015[6]).

Recommendations

Generally, satisfaction with currently available career guidance services is high and perceived outcomes are strong, even if most adults do not directly attribute those outcomes to career guidance. Still, there are many ways that the quality of services could be improved. Competence frameworks, which standardise what career guidance advisors should know and do, are not yet in place in Latin America and quality standards around service delivery are rare. The quality of public career guidance services also varies significantly across local employment offices in the countries reviewed.

- **Strengthen general public service delivery quality standards and include a component that considers career guidance specifically.**

Further, countries should initiate national consultations to build a competence framework for career guidance advisors (see Chapter 6).

To be effective, guidance should be personalised. In Latin American countries, many adults are in informal employment and lack formal qualifications. Skills profiling tools can be extremely useful in this context to assess what adults can do, but they are not widely used in Latin America. Such a tool would help the advisor to assess what adults can actually do, and could be used as a starting point for making personalised recommendations about training and job pathways.

- **Develop a skills profiling tool that can be used by providers, particularly when working with adults who have no formal qualifications.**

References

Dodd, V. et al. (2019), *Quality Assurance Standards: A synthesis of quality standards across partner countries*, Erasmus, http://guidancequality.eu/quality-assurance-standards-a-synthesis-of-quality-standards-across-partner-countries/. [4]

ILO (2015), *Public Employment Services in Latin America: Argentina*, ILO Notes, https://www.ilo.org/wcmsp5/groups/public/---ed_emp/---emp_policy/---cepol/documents/publication/wcms_426610.pdf (accessed on 22 January 2021). [5]

Joana Silva, R. (2015), *Sustaining Employment and Wage Gains in Brazil - A Skills and Jobs Agenda*, The World Bank, https://openknowledge.worldbank.org/bitstream/handle/10986/22545/9781464806445.pdf;sequence=5. [6]

OECD (2021). *Career Guidance for Adults in a Changing World of Work*, OECD Publishing, Paris, https://www.oecd-ilibrary.org/employment/career-guidance-for-adults-in-a-changing-world-of-work_9a94bfad-en (accessed on 8 January 2021). [7]

OECD (2021). *Career Guidance for Adults in a Changing World of Work*, Getting Skills Right, OECD Publishing, Paris, https://dx.doi.org/10.1787/9a94bfad-en. [3]

OECD (2020). "Career guidance for adults", *137th Session of the Employment, Labour and Social Affairs Committee (ELSAC).* [2]

Wilcock, C. (2021), *Comparing Apples to Pommes: Understanding and Accounting for Cultural Bias in Global B2B Research*, https://www.b2binternational.com/publications/understanding-accounting-cultural-bias-global-b2b-research/ (accessed on 1 February 2021). [1]

Note

[1] In Chile, the Holland Test and Prediger Test are used to narrow down interests and preferences. Other tests assess the individual's personality type (e.g. DISC test, Catell's 16 Factor Personality Test, Personality Inventory for Salespeople, MBTI Personality Indicator).

6 Governance and funding

Ministries, public bodies, local governments and the social partners share responsibilities for adult career guidance policy in Latin America. Where strong coordination mechanisms are in place, they facilitate policy development as well as the provision of high-quality services. This chapter sketches how the actors governing career guidance in Latin America coordinate with one another. It also discusses how costs for career guidance are divided between government, employers and adults. It suggests ways to reduce the cost of career guidance services for those individuals who cannot afford them.

In Brief

Effective co-ordination for sustainable governance and funding of adult career guidance in Latin America

The governance of career guidance for adults is often distributed across different levels of government. To ensure good co-ordination between them, strong mechanisms need to be in place that facilitate the exchange of information and the complementarity of guidance services. The cost of services is typically shared between individuals and public authorities. The main findings from this chapter are:

- The Ministry of Labour has the lead on governance of career guidance for adults in Argentina, Brazil and Chile, whereas in Mexico it is the Ministry of Education. In all four countries, there is close cooperation with the national public employment service (PES).

- In most Latin American countries, legislative and policy design powers lie within the respective national ministry but given their decentralised systems, regional or local governments have certain autonomy in implementing and adapting regulations to the local context.

- Several countries have set up tripartite bodies or councils that engage the social partners in policy making processes and the governance of career guidance programmes. They may be responsible for the recognition of prior learning, the validation and certification of skills, or the development of strategies to meet training needs in line with employment demand.

- Adults are more likely to pay out-of-pocket for career guidance in Latin America compared with other countries in the SCGA. In Argentina and Mexico, almost half (45%) of users reported having paid for the service they chose. In Brazil, 40% bear the cost themselves, as does a third of users in Chile. This compares with only 31% of adult users in all countries covered by the survey.

- Those who are unemployed, inactive, self-employed or on temporary contracts are more likely to pay out-of-pocket for career support in Latin America compared with in other countries in the survey, This suggests that cost is a larger barrier for the inclusiveness of career guidance in these countries.

- As in other countries, employers, especially bigger companies, provide career guidance free of charge in certain contexts in Latin America. Employers may provide support for key talent groups to organise their career development and at the same time promote productivity and employee retention, or they may provide outplacement services to laid off workers in order to meet legal requirements.

Introduction

Responsibilities for adult career guidance are shared across ministries, specialised public bodies, levels of government as well as social partners and other stakeholders. Good co-ordination mechanisms can help to implement coherent career guidance policy, facilitate seamless and high-quality service delivery, and avoid gaps in provision. As career guidance has both public and private benefits, different measures of cost-sharing between government, employers and individuals can help to establish a sustainable model of funding.

The first section of this chapter reviews how career guidance is governed in the Latin American countries under study. It examines horizontal co-ordination across ministries and other public bodies, vertical co-ordination across different levels of government as well as the involvement of other stakeholders. The next section looks at the role of career guidance strategies at promoting co-ordination. Lastly, the chapter discusses how the costs for career guidance are shared among adults, employers and governments.

How is career guidance governed in Latin America?

Responsibility for governing public career guidance is often divided across different ministries and levels of government, so good co-ordination between these stakeholders is key. Social partners and professional associations are also involved in decision-making on career guidance. This section describes the co-ordination mechanisms used in the Latin American countries examined, horizontally and vertically within government, as well as with social partners.

Horizontal co-ordination between ministries

Career guidance for adults is at the nexus of employment and education policy, and responsibilities tends to be split between ministries and public bodies. This is different from career guidance for young people, which generally falls under the responsibility of the Ministry of Education. Across the Latin American countries in the SCGA, most often it is the Ministry of Labour, in co-operation with the PES, who is involved in governing career guidance policy for adults. Together, these public authorities have jurisdiction over the career guidance services directed at unemployed people or at-risk workers to help them find a job or improve their employability. **Mexico** is an exception, where the Ministry of Education has the main responsibility for career guidance. In **Chile**, the Ministry of Social Development (*Ministerio de Desarrollo Social, MIDES*) is additionally involved in specific career guidance programmes targeted at vulnerable populations.

Good horizontal co-ordination between ministries and other public bodies with responsibility related to career guidance is key. Co-ordination can be enforced by legislation, be delegated to a permanent national-level advisory body or take place in less formal working groups. In some countries, there are specialised bodies, usually subordinated to a ministry, with particular responsibilities in the area of training, skills and employability, where co-ordination of guidance services is part of the mandate. In **Chile**, the National Training and Employment Service SENCE (*Servicio Nacional de Capacitación y Empleo*) runs different training and employment programmes, supervises the municipal employment offices *(Oficinas Municipales de Intermediación Laboral, OMIL)* and steers activities related to career guidance in Chile. The **Mexican** National Council for Educational Development (*Consejo Nacional de Fomento Educativo*, CONAFE) is a public body of the federal government dedicated to the educational and skill development of people from marginalised communities, including indigenous youth and adults, migrant workers and those living in rural areas.

To date, however, there is no dedicated working group, permanent advisory body or public authority responsible for career guidance as a separate policy area in Latin American countries. Such a body exists in the **Czech Republic**, for example, where the Ministry of Education and the Ministry of Labour jointly established the National Guidance Forum (NGF) as an advisory body in 2010. Through working groups and project partnerships, the NGF promotes inter-ministerial co-ordination on the career guidance policy. **Ireland** has a dedicated National Centre for Guidance in Education (NCGE), with responsibility to support and develop guidance practices and to inform national guidance policy. The centre works with key stakeholders to promote quality standards, innovative approaches, and professional development for career guidance advisors. In a similar vein, **Germany's** National Forum for Educational, Vocational and Employment-oriented Guidance (*Nationales Forum Beratung, Beruf, und Beschäftigung*) provides a national platform for knowledge exchange, co-operation and quality development (OECD, 2021[1]).

Experiences from these and other countries show that a co-ordinated, systematic approach can strengthen the quality of public services and avoid gaps in the provision of career guidance.

Vertical co-ordination between levels of government

Typically, central, regional and municipal levels of government share responsibility for the governance of career guidance. Three out of four countries, including Argentina, Brazil and Chile, have decentralised systems. In these systems, the national government has a steering role and designs the policy, while the regional or local governments are responsible for implementing career guidance. Mexico is an exception, where the national government is responsible for both the design and implementation of career guidance.

Each approach comes with advantages and disadvantages. Centralised career guidance systems benefit from clear responsibility and leadership, but might experience a gap between national and local priorities or poor local implementation. More decentralised systems often have a better alignment of policy planning and application, which can lead to effective career guidance provision adapted to local need. The pitfall of a decentralised approach is a lack of co-ordination, e.g. due to a slow or absent information flow, or to diverging political priorities between the different levels of government. Decentralised career guidance systems generally entail a greater risk of asymmetries in funding and quality of public providers across the country.

Countries have different ways to co-ordinate career guidance activities across national, regional and municipal levels of government. One approach is to pair centralised policy steering with local implementation. Some countries choose to have working groups or steering committees that support and overlook vertical co-ordination of career guidance across all levels of government. In addition, formal pathways to share information on career guidance can support co-ordination across different levels of government. Argentina, Brazil and Mexico do not have strong mechanisms in place to promote vertical co-ordination, but Chile provides a good example of a well-co-ordinated system of governance with integrated service provision (Box 6.1).

In Chile, the National Training and Employment Service SENCE (*Servicio Nacional de Capacitación y Empleo*), under the authority of the Labour Ministry, is responsible for the design and monitoring of the country's career guidance activities. As part of the larger strategy on labour intermediation and employment policy, local governments are responsible for implementing career guidance activities through municipal employment offices (*Oficinas Municipales de Intermediación Laboral, OMIL*).

SENCE maintains a close relationship with the OMIL based on a collaborative system of financial incentives as well as legal agreements. SENCE provides funds according to a number of indicators, such as the number of counselling sessions, successful job placements or trainings provided. The OMILs receive regular technical assistance through Regional Directorates, which, in turn, are monitored by the SENCE head office. The regular two-way information exchange helps the central government to understand local needs when designing policies for career guidance.

In addition, the National Jobs Portal (*Bolsa Nacional de Empleo, BNE*) is SENCE's digital system for managing labour intermediation services. It provides labour market information for jobseekers, employers and institutions. Moreover, individuals can retrieve online advice about employment programs, training opportunities as well as career guidance. All clients of the OMIL have to register on the portal and receive instructions on how to use it. Some challenge remain, such as a lack of funding and staff in the OMILs, inequalities in service provision across municipal employment offices, as well as a strong focus on job placement rather than the sustainability and quality of job matches. Nevertheless, SENCE, the OMIL and the BNE together form a good example of a well-co-ordinated system of governance with integrated service provision of career guidance in Chile.

Source: OECD Secretariat, OECD 2020 Policy Questionnaire 'Career Guidance for Adults'.

Engaging stakeholders in setting career guidance policy

Latin American countries employ different approaches to engage key stakeholders in career guidance policy. A common way to engage social partners, is to include them in advisory bodies to co-ordinate and steer employment policy, which often includes responsibility for career guidance. An example in Latin America is the tripartite Advisory Board of the Worker's Support Fund (*Conselho Deliberativo do Fundo de Amparo ao Trabalhador, CODEFAT*) of the **Brazilian** Ministry of Economy, which involves representatives of government, labour unions and employers. The CODEFAT is the competent body for labour intermediation and employment policies. It is responsible for allocating resources, designing guidelines for programmes, monitoring and evaluating their social impact, as well as proposing improvements in policy legislation (Ministério da Economia, 2021[2]).

In several countries, independent, tripartite public bodies have specific responsibility for the certification of skills and setting competence standards. Examples are *CONOCER* in **Mexico**, *ChileValora* in **Chile** as well as the Sectorial Councils for Job Skills Certification and Training (*Consejos Sectoriales de Formación y Certificación de Competencias Laborales y Formación Profesional*) in **Argentina**. These are institutions that develop strategies to meet training needs in line with employment demand, and to strengthen vocational training institutions for particular sectors. The councils are organised by the Ministry of Labour and involve state, business, and labour union representatives (Bertranou, 2014[3]).

The governance of these bodies is tripartite, and consists of representatives of workers, employers, as well as government. In addition, employers and chambers of commerce are consulted about the skills necessary in each sector in order to develop competence standards and to better align training and standards of certification of skills with local and sectoral labour market demand. While these bodies may only partially be involved in career guidance as such, they are important stakeholders in national skills development systems. Their activities interlink with career guidance providers as they provide important information, set standards and create the connection between training, education and certification.

There are also examples of sector-specific stakeholder engagement in career guidance. The UOCRA Foundation in **Argentina**, to name one, brings together the Union of Construction Workers of the Argentine Republic (UOCRA) and the Argentine Chamber of Construction (CAC) to promote training, education and competency standards for construction workers. Other stakeholders involved in the UOCRA Foundation are the Statistics and Records Institute, the Sectoral Council for Certification of Competencies and Vocational Training as well as the Argentinian Government. While not focusing on career guidance in particular, the aim of the initiative is to promote a strategic, sector-level approach to the skills development of construction workers (EFT, CEDEFOP and ILO, 2016[4]).

In addition to the social partners, professional associations are important stakeholders in the governance of career guidance in many countries. They can support professional training of career counsellors, exchange best practices, develop guidelines and standards and provide expertise to governments. Although some professional associations exist in Latin American countries, for example the Fundación OCIDES in **Chile** or the Brazilian Association of Career Guidance *(ABOP)* in **Brazil**, to date they have little influence on the governance of career guidance. The knowledge and resources these actors have developed warrants their inclusion into decision-making on career guidance policy, for example as part of national stakeholder groups or advisory bodies.

Box 6.2. Career guidance associations in Latin America

The **Fundación OCIDES** is a Chilean organisation that promotes the practice of career guidance and implements projects and activities to strengthen the community of guidance professionals in Chile. Its activities include institutional capacity-building, workshops and trainings for career guidance advisors, the dissemination of publications and other resources on career guidance, as well as advocacy for public policies on lifelong learning, such as a national strategy on career guidance.

The **Brazilian Association of Career Guidance** (*ABOP – Associação Brasileira de Orientação Profissional*) connects guidance professionals, and promotes research in the field. While not providing career guidance as such, they also organise different activities to share knowledge and raise awareness about its value in the Brazilian context. ABOP is affiliated with the International Association of Educational and Vocational Guidance (IAEVG).

Source: Fundanción OCIDES (2021[5]), https://www.ocides.org/ (accessed on 15 January 2021); ABOP (2021[6]), *Associação Brasileira de Orientação Profissional*, https://abopbrasil.org.br/ (accessed on 15 January 2021).

What is the role of career guidance strategies in Latin America?

A career guidance strategy sets out the vision, objectives and priorities for action in the area of career guidance. Ideally, it describes career guidance across different contexts, including who is responsible for providing career guidance, eligibility, quality mechanisms and funding. In those OECD countries that have career guidance strategies, they are often embedded in a wider lifelong learning or skills strategy, as career guidance is often viewed as crucial for the success of lifelong learning and employment strategies (Barnes et al., 2020[7]; OECD, 2017[8]). Only a few countries have stand-alone career guidance strategies (Greece, Italy, Korea, and Turkey). The success of such strategies is supported by the involvement of all relevant stakeholders during their creation, by defined sources of funding for career guidance, as well as quantitative targets that allow the evaluation and monitoring of outcomes (OECD, 2021[1]). A national strategy that specifically considers career guidance provides leadership to all actors in the system, and can help to build policy coherence.

Career guidance strategies are not common in Latin American countries. None of the Latin American countries studied has a coherent and dedicated guidance strategy to channel and co-ordinate career guidance activities. **Mexico** has a career guidance strategy for youth, with the aim of helping young people to take career choices after high-school graduation, but there is no career guidance strategy for adults. Service provision in **Argentinian** PES follow a larger government strategy on employment policy that covers matters of labour policy, occupational qualifications, and training programs, without a particular focus on career guidance. While it does not have a dedicated national career guidance or skills strategy per se, the **Chilean** National Training and Employment Service SENCE sets out policy priorities for labour intermediation services, with specific guidelines for local PES, and monitors indicators such as the number of counselling sessions, successful job placements or trainings provided.

How is career guidance for adults funded in Latin America?

The discussion about who benefits from and thus who should pay for career guidance is ongoing (see OECD (2021[9])). In Latin America, there are two main sources of funding: public funding and out-of-pocket payments by individuals. Career guidance provided by the PES is mostly publicly funded and free of charge for all eligible individuals. The more time- and resource-intensive career guidance by private providers is fully paid by the individual. To a more limited extent, there are private non-profit organisations and universities that provide career guidance free of charge, for instance to vulnerable or low-income populations (see Chapter 4). Employers tend to provide guidance to their employees as well, but little is known in the Latin American context. As private providers are the most frequently used providers in Latin America (see Chapter 4), taking up career guidance services might be prohibitively costly for many individuals.

Career guidance serves adults, as it supports their progression in learning and work. Guidance also yields public benefits, however, and firms can profit from the skill development of their employees as well. Although cross-country data on the funding of career guidance is scarce, there is a wide range of examples for policies in OECD countries that support adequate funding and cost-sharing between individuals, firms and the government. In **Flanders** (Belgium), employees receive training vouchers that can also be used for career guidance sessions. Individuals can purchase up to EUR 250 in training vouchers per calendar year, and the Flemish Government funds half of it. In certain cases, additional financial support can be requested. In **France**, employers fund the *compte personnel de formation* (CPF, Individual Training Account) via a levy on medium and large-sized firms (OECD, 2019[10]), which can also be used to pay for career guidance services, such as conducting a skills assessment. In the **Netherlands**, a pilot programme targeted subsidies for career guidance at vulnerable groups of employed adults. The subsidy was available for career guidance services to persons aged 45+ who worked at least 12 hours per week (*Ontwikkeladvies*). The pilot is currently under evaluation.

Adults' out-of-pocket spending

Career guidance can generate private returns for individuals depending on their individual situation and prospects for their professional life. Users may value the positive psychological effects of career guidance, such as higher self-esteem, self-confidence or insight, awareness of opportunities, and motivation (Kidd, Jackson and Hirsh, 2003[11]; Bimrose and Brown, 2019[12]). They may also value the opportunity to learn new skills, such as decision-making and information-seeking skills (Maguire, 2004[13]). These benefits motivate many adults to invest in guidance, and explains the substantial level of individual contributions.

None of the Latin American countries in the study offer any schemes to promote co-funding of private career guidance between individuals and the government. This lack of co-funding schemes is a notable difference compared with other countries covered by the SCGA, where either public career guidance is used more or private career guidance is subsidised. In Latin America, the full cost of private services is thus often borne by the individual, which hinders access for those who cannot afford it. This concerns not only the direct costs for the guidance services, but also the opportunity costs associated with taking time away from work to speak with a career guidance advisor. Career guidance provided by the PES is free of charge in all Latin American countries, but as outlined in Chapter 3, it is not used as much, and not all adults are eligible for it.

The share of adults who paid for career guidance services is consequently higher in Latin America than the overall SCGA average, except for Chile (Figure 6.1). In Argentina, Brazil and Mexico 40-45% of adults paid for their guidance services, compared with the overall average of 31%. In Chile, this percentage is slightly below average (30%). The lower percentage of users paying for guidance in Chile may be due to the higher offer of free career guidance services compared with the other three Latin American countries. These findings are not surprising given the prevalence of private and fee-based career guidance services in Latin America (see Chapter 4).

The findings are problematic for inclusiveness, however, as vulnerable groups, such as the unemployed or low-skilled adults, face barriers to access quality guidance services (see Chapter 3). Figure 6.2 shows that even though unemployed adults are less likely than employed adults (permanent, temporary, self-employed or informal) to pay out-of-pocket for career support in Latin America, they are much more likely to pay compared with other countries in the survey.

Figure 6.1. Adults' out-of-pocket contribution to career guidance

Percentage of adult career guidance users who paid (partially or fully) for services

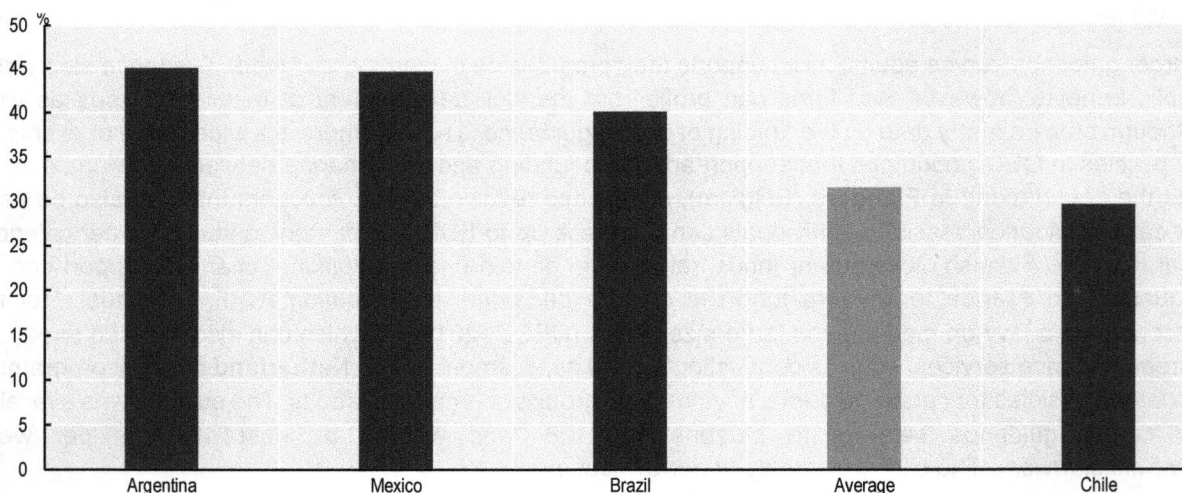

Note: Average includes Argentina, Brazil, Chile, France, Germany, Italy, Mexico, New Zealand and the United States. Data refers to the last time the respondent spoke to a career guidance advisor.
Source: OECD 2020 Survey of Career Guidance for Adults (SCGA).

Figure 6.2. Adults' out-of-pocket contribution to career guidance, by employment status

Percentage of adult career guidance users who paid (partially or fully) for services, by employment status

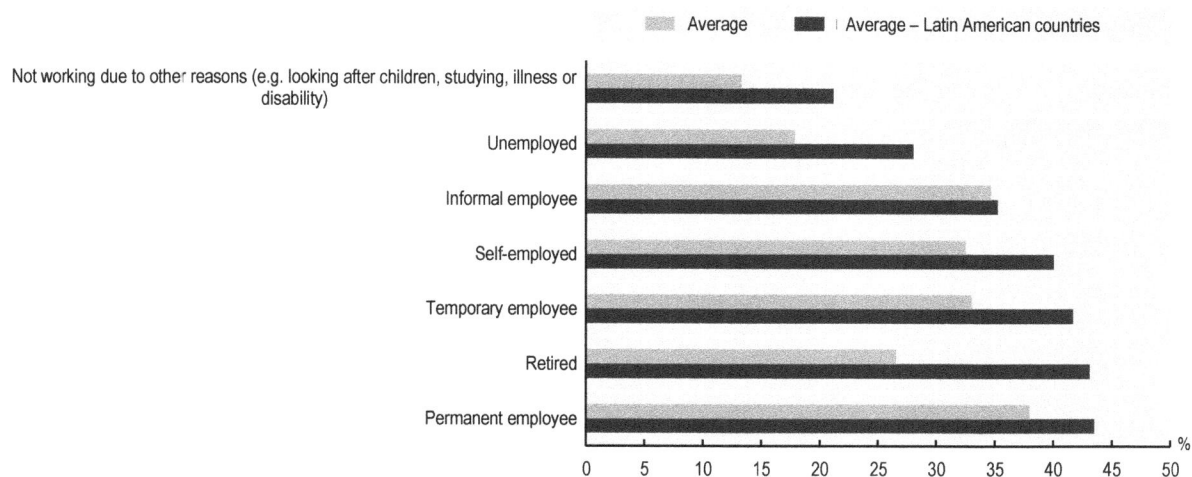

Note: Average – Latin American countries includes Argentina, Brazil, Chile and Mexico. Average includes Argentina, Brazil, Chile, France, Germany, Italy, Mexico, New Zealand and the United States.
Source: OECD 2020 Survey of Career Guidance for Adults (SCGA).

Government contribution to funding

Governments have an interest in contributing to well-functioning and effective career guidance for individuals and companies, considering the substantial benefits of guidance for economies and societies as a whole (OECD, 2004[14]; OECD, 2021[1]). Public funding is crucial for broadening access to vulnerable individuals who are less likely to seek guidance on their own initiative, or who could otherwise not afford the costs. Public funding of career guidance during economic crises, such as the current COVID-19 pandemic, can help to smooth the business cycle and facilitate structural adjustment by helping individuals to transition to new jobs and sectors.

With no financial incentives in place that go directly to an individual or company, all public funding for career guidance in Latin America is invested directly in the services provided by the PES or other public guidance providers. Most funding comes from the Ministry of Labour (Argentina, Brazil,[1] Chile) and is then distributed to the PES offices in the different municipalities or regions. In Mexico, public funding comes from the Secretariat of Labour and Social Security, which co-ordinates the national PES in co-operation with the federal states.

Some countries have public funds dedicated to employment policy, parts of which can be used for career guidance activities or programmes (*Fondo Nacional de Empleo* in **Argentina**, *Fundo de Amparo ao Trabalhador, FAT* in **Brazil**). The Brazilian FAT's resources come from taxes paid by individuals and firms.

Estimates of national PES funding in each of the four countries are difficult to obtain, often out of date and not directly comparable. A large share of PES funding is usually dedicated to services other than career guidance, including training provision or passive benefits such as unemployment insurance. Furthermore, definitions of career guidance vary, and public providers focus on different types of services, programmes as well as target groups. Nevertheless, available data suggests that there is considerable variation in public funding across the countries in this review (see Table 3.1 in Chapter 4). As a result, funding levels for public or publicly subsidised career guidance services are also likely to differ.

Employers' contribution to funding

Little is known about employers' contribution to the funding of career guidance activities in Latin America. Companies' interest in investing in the skills of their employees include increasing productivity, maintaining competitiveness and fostering innovation. When legally required, such as for instance in **Mexico**, employers must finance outplacement services to help laid-off employees find a new job or start up their own business. In some sectors, employers' associations offer career guidance financed through companies' contributions.

Recommendations

The primary responsibility of public career guidance for adults tends to be with the Ministry of Labour or the Ministry of Education in Latin American countries, with co-operation from the PES. The social partners are often involved in the governance of public bodies with general responsibility for training and employment. However, in none of the Latin American country studied is there a dedicated policy strategy on career guidance. Ideally, such an approach would involve all relevant stakeholders; that is, the public authorities, the social partners and professional guidance associations. The knowledge and resources of each of these actors is valuable and could be better integrated into decision-making. Efforts to enhance the quality of services, and to develop competence frameworks for career guidance advisors, for example, would greatly benefit from a broad, collaborative approach.

- **Consider forming a working group with all relevant stakeholders to improve career guidance policy and provision.**

Typically, regional governments are responsible for the implementation of career guidance in Latin America. In some of the countries in this review, co-ordination between the different levels of government and other public bodies responsible for career guidance could be improved. An established flow of information in both directions can create accountability, and helps to keep track of outcomes. This has the potential to improve career guidance services, and entrench good co-operation mechanisms that work independently of the political leadership in place. It may also be useful to organise regular international exchanges of good practice and promising initiatives across Latin American countries.

- **Develop a system of regular reporting standards between local employment offices, national ministries and other relevant public bodies, and facilitate international exchanges of good practice.**

Compared with other countries, in Latin America adults are more likely to pay out-of-pocket for career guidance. This hints at a limited availability of subsidised or free guidance, which is particularly a challenge for unemployed, informal and inactive workers, who tend to be more vulnerable in the labour market and are less able to afford these costs. To support the accessibility and uptake of career guidance services by these adults, adequate funding for public career guidance services – such as those delivered by the PES – is needed. This is especially the case during a period of major economic disruption, as with the current COVID-19 crisis.

Adults could benefit from support to cover both the direct and indirect costs of public and private career guidance services. Measures could take the form of vouchers, subsidies or income support to account for opportunity costs associated with taking time away from work to speak with a career guidance advisor. Another way would be to review the unemployment support system to enable jobseekers to invest time in career guidance, without feeling pressure to quickly find a job to feed their families. Designing such a policy requires a comprehensive analysis of factors that would improve take-up, taking into account the provider landscape as well as social security provisions.

- **Design financial measures to reduce the direct and indirect costs of career guidance for vulnerable adults.**

References

ABOP (2021), *Associação Brasileira de Orientação Profissional.*, https://abopbrasil.org.br/ (accessed on 15 January 2021). [6]

Barnes, S. et al. (2020), *Lifelong guidance policy and practice in the EU: trends, challenges and opportunities*, European Commission, http://dx.doi.org/10.2767/91185. [7]

Bertranou, F. (2014), *Employment policy implementation mechanisms in Argentina*, ILO, http://www.ilo.org/publns (accessed on 29 January 2021). [3]

Bimrose, J., S. Barnes and D. Hughes (2008), *Adult career progression & advancement: a five year study of the effectiveness of guidance*, Institute for Employment Research, University of Warwick, https://warwick.ac.uk/fac/soc/ier/publications/2008/eg_report_4_years_on_final.pdf (accessed on 29 January 2021). [26]

Bimrose, J. and A. Brown (2019), "Professional identity transformation: supporting career and employment practitioners at a distance", *British Journal of Guidance & Counselling*, Vol. 47/6, pp. 757-769, http://dx.doi.org/10.1080/03069885.2019.1698008. [12]

CODEFAT (n.d.), *CODEFAT – Portal do Fundo de Amparo ao Trabalhador*, https://portalfat.mte.gov.br/codefat/ (accessed on 27 November 2020). [19]

EFT, CEDEFOP and ILO (2016), *Working at sectoral level: Guide to anticipating and matching skills and jobs. Volume 3*, http://dx.doi.org/10.2816/421107. [4]

Fundación OCIDES (2021), *Fundación OCIDES. Desarrollo de carrera y orientación a lo largo de la vida*, https://www.ocides.org/ (accessed on 15 January 2021). [5]

Helbig, D., R. Mazzola and M. García (2015), *Servicios Públicos de Empleo en Argentina como pilar de apoyo a la política de empleo*, International Labour Organization, https://www.ilo.org/wcmsp5/groups/public/---americas/---ro-lima/---ilo-buenos_aires/documents/publication/wcms_452861.pdf (accessed on 13 January 2021). [18]

IDB, W. (2015), *The World of Public Employment Services. Challenges, capacity and outlook for public employment services in the new world of work.*, https://doi.org/10.1787/9789264251854-en (accessed on 15 January 2021). [21]

ILO (2015), *Public Employment Services in Latin America and the Caribbean. Chile.*, https://www.ilo.org/wcmsp5/groups/public/---ed_emp/---emp_policy/---cepol/documents/publication/wcms_434598.pdf (accessed on 13 January 2021). [23]

Kidd, J., C. Jackson and W. Hirsh (2003), "The outcomes of effective career discussion at work", *Journal of Vocational Behavior*, Vol. 62/1, pp. 119-133, http://dx.doi.org/10.1016/s0001-8791(02)00027-1. [11]

Maguire, M. (2004), "Measuring the Outcomes of Career Guidance", *International Journal for Educational and Vocational Guidance*, Vol. 4/2-3, pp. 179-192, http://dx.doi.org/10.1007/s10775-005-1022-1. [13]

México, G. (2021), *Servicio Nacional de Empleo*, Estadísticas Laborales, https://www.empleo.gob.mx/sne (accessed on 13 January 2021). [25]

Ministério da Economia (2021), *CODEFAT – Portal do Fundo de Amparo ao Trabalhador*, [2]
https://portalfat.mte.gov.br/codefat/ (accessed on 29 January 2021).

Ministério da Economia (2016), *Estatísticas SINE – Portal do Fundo de Amparo ao Trabalhador*, [17]
http://portalfat.mte.gov.br/programas-e-acoes-2/sistema-nacional-de-emprego-sine/rede-
sine/estatisticas-sine/ (accessed on 13 January 2021).

Ministry of Labour, E. (2021), *Programas de empleo y capacitación*, [22]
http://www.trabajo.gob.ar/estadisticas/Bel/programas.asp (accessed on 13 January 2021).

OECD (2021), *Career Guidance for Adults in a Changing World of Work*, OECD Publishing, [9]
Paris, https://www.oecd-ilibrary.org/employment/career-guidance-for-adults-in-a-changing-
world-of-work_9a94bfad-en (accessed on 8 January 2021).

OECD (2021), *Career Guidance for Adults in a Changing World of Work*, Getting Skills Right, [1]
OECD Publishing, Paris, https://dx.doi.org/10.1787/9a94bfad-en.

OECD (2020), "Career guidance for adults", *137th Session of the Employment, Labour and* [20]
Social Affairs Committee (ELSAC).

OECD (2019), *Individual Learning Accounts : Panacea or Pandora's Box?*, OECD Publishing, [27]
Paris, https://dx.doi.org/10.1787/203b21a8-en.

OECD (2019), *Individual Learning Accounts: Panacea or Pandora's Box?*, OECD Publishing, [10]
Paris, https://www.oecd-ilibrary.org/employment/individual-learning-schemes_203b21a8-en
(accessed on 4 February 2021).

OECD (2017), *Financial Incentives for Steering Education and Training*, Getting Skills Right, [8]
OECD Publishing, Paris, https://dx.doi.org/10.1787/9789264272415-en.

OECD (2004), *Career Guidance and Public Policy. Bridging the Gap*, [14]
http://www.SourceOECD.org, (accessed on 25 January 2021).

OECD (2004), *Career Guidance and Public Policy: Bridging The Gap*. [15]

SENCE (2020), *Intermediación Laboral año 2020*, http://www.sence.cl/601/articles- [16]
14036_archivo_04.pdf (accessed on 13 January 2021).

Servicio Nacional de Empleo (2021), *Cobertura del SNE | Portal del Empleo*, [24]
https://www.empleo.gob.mx/sne/cobertura (accessed on 13 January 2021).

Note

[1] In Brazil, there is no Ministry of Labour, but rather a Labour Secretariat linked to the Ministry of Economy.

Annex A. Methodology note on Survey of Career Guidance for Adults

This report uses data collected in the 2020 Survey of Career Guidance for Adults (SCGA). The SCGA was conducted to better understand adults' experience with career guidance services and to improve international data on coverage.

Fieldwork was conducted by Cint[1] in two phases using an online questionnaire developed by the OECD. The first phase of fieldwork took place from mid-June to early July 2020 in six countries: Chile, France, Germany, Italy, New Zealand and the United States. The second phase took place in November 2020 in Argentina, Brazil and Mexico.[2] Among the four Latin American countries covered by this report, the Chilean data was thus collected five months earlier than the other three countries' data. The sample was restricted to adults aged 25-64, in order to target those who had left initial education.

The survey was prepared in six languages (English, French, German, Italian, Portuguese and Spanish) and distributed in the country's official language. Cint disseminated the online survey to a "pre-approved" panel of registered users using a stratified sample methodology, which imposed quotas on age, gender and region. This means that Cint drew a sub-sample from its panel that is representative of each country's population in terms of age, gender and region. The age and gender quotas were based on UN World Population Prospects statistics (https://population.un.org/wpp), while the region quotas were based on Cint's own data.

Education quotas were added in the second phase of data collection (i.e. Argentina, Brazil and Mexico). In the first phase, adults with higher levels of education were over-sampled (see Annex in OECD (2021[1]). This is expected to some extent because online surveys tend to over-represent the behaviour of people who are online, who tend to be individuals with higher levels of formal education (Van Der Heyden et al., 2017[2]). However, the oversampling of higher educated adults was much higher in Chile than in the other countries in the first phase of data collection. To avoid such bias with other Latin American countries in the second phase of data collection, quotas on education were applied. Education quotas were based on OECD Education at a Glance.

After data collection, two quality checks were applied. First, if a respondent completed the survey in two minutes or less, the respondent was excluded. This is based on the assumption that the survey takes more than two minutes to complete with appropriate consideration. Second, if a respondent did not answer the final question of the survey, they were also excluded. This was to ensure that only respondents who completed the full survey were captured in the final dataset.

To ensure adequate sample sizes and comparability, the data collection aimed at 1 000 observations per country. Annex Table 1 shows the final sample sizes by country, after sample restrictions, quotas and the quality checks had been applied.

Annex Figure 1 compares the composition of the country-level samples with the composition of the actual population in each country. Thanks to quotas, the sample is very close to the actual population on age and gender in all four countries. The education quotas also ensure that the education profile of the sample is close to that of the actual population in Argentina, Brazil and Mexico. To enable cross-country comparisons, the Chilean data were reweighted wherever the sample size permitted in order to account for over-representation of highly-educated adults. In charts where reweighting of the Chilean data was not possible, a reference can be found in the notes.

Annex Table 1. Final sample size by country

	Sample size
Argentina	1 017
Brazil	964
Chile	959
France	1 075
Germany	921
Italy	982
Mexico	993
New Zealand	904
United States	922

Adults in informal employment are under-represented in the SCGA. Adults who reported being "employed without a contract" – a proxy for informal employment – made up only 7% of employed adults in the sample, while 40% of employed adults find themselves in informal employment in the actual population (CEDLAS and The World Bank, n.d.[3]).

Annex Figure 1. Sample composition by age, gender and education group, compared to actual population

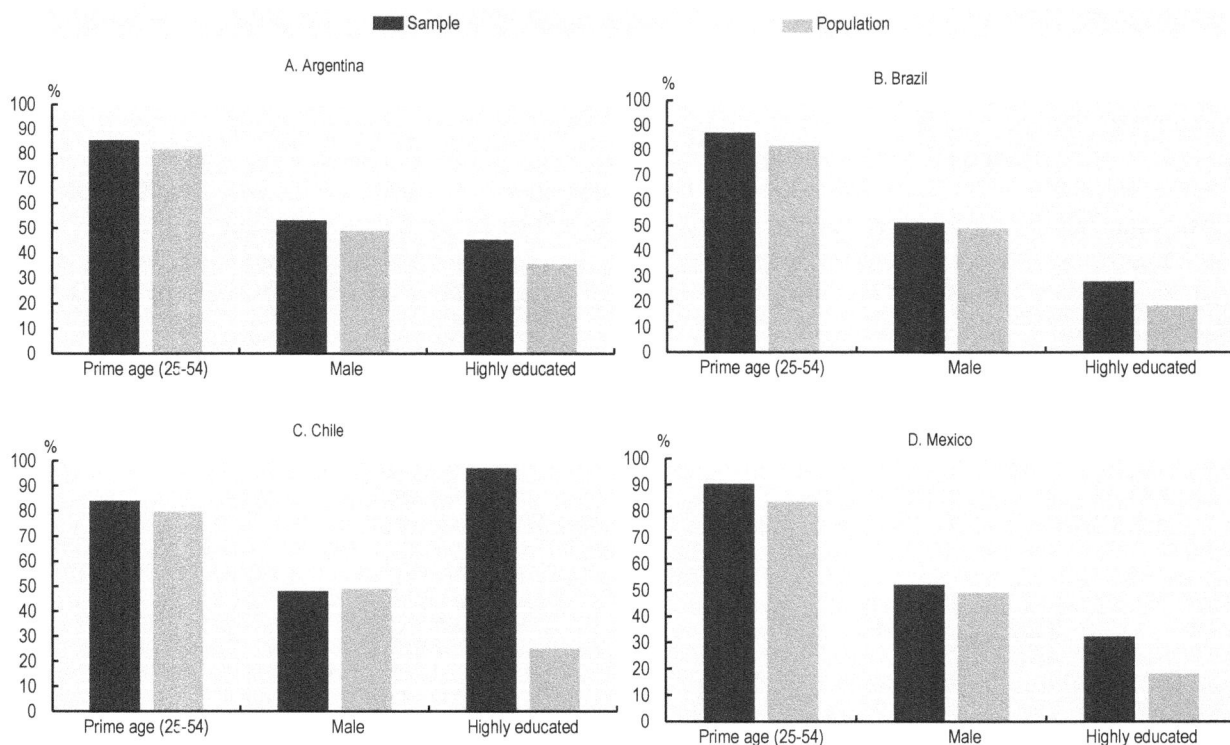

Note: "Highly educated" refers to the share of the population with a tertiary education (ISCED 4-6). The other education groups not shown here. are below upper secondary education (ISCED 0-2), and upper secondary or post-secondary non-tertiary education (ISCED 3).
Source: The sample composition by age, gender and education is drawn from the Survey of Career Guidance for Adults (SCGA). The population. distribution of age and gender were extracted from UN 2019 Revision of World Population Prospects (https://population.un.org/wpp/). For population estimates by education group, OECD Education at a Glance 2020 was used.

References

CEDLAS and The World Bank (n.d.), *SEDLAC Statistics*, [3]
https://www.cedlas.econo.unlp.edu.ar/wp/en/estadisticas/sedlac/estadisticas/#149616550997
5-36a05fb8-428b (accessed on 3 December 2020).

OECD (2021), *Career Guidance for Adults in a Changing World of Work*, Getting Skills Right, [1]
OECD Publishing, Paris, https://dx.doi.org/10.1787/9a94bfad-en.

Van Der Heyden, J. et al. (2017), *Additional weighting for education affects estimates from a* [2]
National Health Interview Survey, http://dx.doi.org/10.1093/eurpub/ckx005.

Notes

[1] Cint is a digital insights gathering platform (www.cint.com). The Cint platform and products comply with standards and certifications set out by various market research associations including ESOMAR, MRS, ARF, MRIA, AMA, AMSRO and Insights Association and ISO 20 252 quality standards.

[2] The online survey was conducted in June-July and November 2020, in the middle of the COVID-19 crisis. One implication of this is that more people were able to respond to the survey because they were confined at home, were teleworking, and/or because they lost their job and had more time available. Cint noted that response rates were higher than expected as a result. Any impact this might have had on sample composition, however, was mitigated by the use of quotas. Countries were also at different stages of the pandemic when the survey was conducted. It is possible that policy measures adopted in different countries to cope with COVID-19 could have indirectly influenced the use of career guidance services. For instance, those countries that were more heavily affected by the pandemic at the time of the survey may have had more people out of work or at risk of losing their job as a result of the policy measures that were adopted (e.g. temporary business closures, travel restrictions). This could have affected the share of people who used career guidance services.